Published by
Silicon Valley Press

Fans Have More Friends

Ben Valenta
David Sikorjak

Foreword by Michael Mulvihill		9
Introduction		15
01	Reframing Fandom	35
02	Fans Have More Friends	59
03	The Fandom Flywheel	83
04	The Benefits of Belonging	111
05	The Polarization Problem	129
06	Fandom as Identity	165
07	Embrace Your Fandom	183
Notes		198
Acknowledgments		200

Foreword
by Michael Mulvihill

A kid in a cap, wearing a glove, eating ice cream at his first Major League game. Three generations of Crimson Tide fans together on a crisp autumn Saturday. A group of boisterous friends in the prime of life cheering on the Packers at Lambeau Field. A couple on a first date at Dodger Stadium, not knowing much about each other except their shared passion for the team.

The most important moments in sports are not happening on the field. They are happening in the stands.

In the seven years that I've had the privilege of working with Ben Valenta at Fox Sports, the insights that he and David Sikorjak have derived from thousands of interactions with fans have led me to a new and, I believe, more correct understanding of what elevates sports to a unique place in the lives of hundreds of millions of fans.

Through in-person interviews and rigorously designed surveys, Ben and David's research has affirmed again and again that what truly drives our business are the human connections facilitated by sports fandom. Sports binds us more closely to our friends, our families, our schools, our communities. For so many of us it can be challenging to articulate just what these relationships mean in our lives. At its best, the language of fandom says it for us.

Those powerful bonds that are difficult to describe are even harder to quantify, which has long presented a challenge to the business of sports. The traditional metrics of television ratings, attendance, and merchandise sales can provide a rough roadmap, but they're a crude and unsatisfying way of capturing what makes our business special. Here, Ben and David lay out a more robust and direct way of using data to define what has heretofore been largely unmeasurable.

It's become fashionable to speak in reverent tones about "the man in the arena." And surely the athletes whose rare talents and hard work command our attention deserve to be rewarded. But I suggest that our business has traditionally been premised on a kind of hero worship that leaves us — fans and business interests alike — vulnerable to human failings, or to the simple passage of time. Our heroes in sports come and go, but fandom endures. A fifteen-year career with the Boston Red Sox is legendary. Fifteen years as a Boston Red Sox fan is barely the beginning. Fans are forever.

Fandom reaches across generations. It reaches across lifetimes. Each year after the Super Bowl or the World Series, we read new stories of fans in the victorious cities who go to the gravesites of loved ones to leave mementos for a departed fan. Even in death, if you're a fan, you belong.

In these pages, Ben and David write deftly on the power of belonging. We live in an increasingly atomized world. Politics, technology, and most recently the pandemic conspire to drive us ever further apart. Our sense of belonging is damaged. In one dispiriting piece of research cited here, 61% of Americans report feeling lonely, and that was before the pandemic and its literal enforcement of isolation. Sports must be an antidote to loneliness. The leaders of the sports industry must recognize that the ability of sports to provide a feeling of belonging isn't just part of the appeal, but rather the reason this entire business exists at all.

I'll close with a story that's never far from my mind as I think about how Fox Sports can be a smarter and more successful business. In 2011, at halftime of Super Bowl XLV in Dallas, my parents and I met a young man who had traveled from Pittsburgh — my own hometown — to see the Steelers play for the Lombardi Trophy. In addition to the usual gameday gear, he was wearing a pair of heavy leather work boots: not exactly comfortable or necessary for a full day on your feet in a domed stadium.

My dad noticed the boots. The young man explained that they had belonged to his own father, now deceased, who had worn them daily for many years to his job in a western Pennsylvania steel mill.

"I don't know," he said haltingly. "I guess I just wanted him to be here."

These poignant stories play out constantly in arenas and stadiums all over the world. In this book, Ben and David go beyond anecdote to compile those stories and present them in a way that allows us — compels us — to think differently about the nature of sports. Their work reminds us of the essential animating quality of fandom: We're in this together.

Introduction

Back in 2018, we sat with lifelong Chicago Cubs fans Nick Camfield and his dad, Lindsay, along the first-base line at Wrigley Field. The setting was postcard perfect, with a field so green you'd think Crayola had created it. The conversation flowed freely between baseball and life. Both Nick and Lindsay are thoughtful and eloquent, blessed with an uncanny ability to wax poetic about baseball's subtle nuances. At some point during the early innings, Nick described a notion so vividly that his words still echo in our minds. He said, "Baseball is my family sport because whenever I see pictures of Ernie Banks, I think of my dad. Whenever I see Ron Santo clicking his heels, I think of my dad in the summers when I was little, watching TV, me sitting on his lap."

What Nick hit on — and what feels relatable to so many sports fans — is that the Cubs are somehow more than just his team. We asked Nick to elaborate on this notion: What does it mean for baseball to be his "family sport"? "Some of my earliest memories are sitting in the living room, playing with my baseball cards while my dad had WGN on the television," he said. "Whenever I hear Harry Caray's voice, it immediately makes me think of childhood, growing up in central Illinois. 'Home' is the only way I can describe it. I feel like everything in the world is where it's supposed to be."

Like that of so many families, the Camfields' loyalty to their team runs at least three generations deep. "It's like a religion, an heirloom that's passed on," Nick said. It didn't matter that the Cubs were known less for winning than for losing spectacularly. "That was just part of who we were," Nick shrugged. "You expected that they were going to play hard, and then they were going to fall short."

The Cubs' tendency to lose, in fact, was part of Nick and Lindsay's bond: "This was what my father suffered through, and his father suffered through, and you know what? I'm going to suffer through it, too, because it's been passed off to me," said Nick. "This has been given to me to take care of, like it's been taken care of before."

Of course, all that changed in 2016. That's when the Cubs won their first World Series in 108 years. Nick, who was a season ticket holder at the time, took his father to a game.

Now, watching any game at Wrigley — much less a World Series game — is a special experience. It transports you. You sense the history. You feel the nostalgia. If you've been there, then you understand firsthand what longtime Cubs fan and Pearl Jam front man Eddie Vedder meant when he once told Cubs radio color analyst Ron Coomer, "Every time I walk [toward Wrigley Field], I get the same feeling I did when I was eight years old. There are not many places in the world that are still like that."[1] Wrigley is the perfect backdrop for exploring intergenerational relationships because it has played host to countless intergenerational moments.

We asked Lindsay what, on the surface, seemed like a simple question: What was it like to watch the Cubs in the World Series at Wrigley Field with his son? Tearing up, all he could muster was a three-word response: "It was special."

One might presume those were tears of joy, the result of a long-awaited championship. But it wasn't the thrill of victory that had Lindsay welling up. It was the connection that the Cubs had created between him and his son. That one World Series game, pivotal as it might have been, encapsulated thousands of other meaningful moments, not simply on the field but in *life*: time spent with his son, time spent with his own father, the countless conversations they've all had throughout the years, ostensibly about the Cubs, but actually about so much more. As it turns out, the Cubs mean so much to Nick and Lindsay because of what they *represent* for Nick and Lindsay: a lifetime bond to each other. We had lumps in our throats, too, in that moment, thinking about our own fathers and sons. In hindsight, it wasn't such a simple question after all.

If we had arbitrarily found ourselves seated next to Nick and his dad at Wrigley Field, listening to them reminisce about seasons past, we might simply have enjoyed the familiar tropes and thought no more of it. Sports fans collect nostalgic stories like these.

But we had invited the Camfields to that game with a purpose: As executives in the sports industry, we wanted to understand the underlying motivations driving fan behavior.

This was part of a larger quest that we had been on for some time. Collectively, we have spent twenty-plus years working in the sports business: as executives, marketers, and consultants for clients and employers such as Fox Sports, ESPN, the National Football League, the New York Knicks, and the New York Rangers. Today, Ben is the senior vice president of strategy and analytics at Fox Sports. Dave, formerly the senior vice president of consumer insights and analytics at Madison Square Garden, runs his own consulting agency, called Dexterity.

Our roles are multidisciplinary by nature, both in terms of our skills and the contexts in which we operate. We like to approach the world in ways that borrow equally from sociology, anthropology, psychology, economics, and good old-fashioned street smarts. We like to think broadly and deeply, and always with empathy. What we're best at is connecting the dots. In that sense, our work is something akin to alchemy. Ultimately, we're good at understanding humans and then translating that understanding into a digestible story. Hence this book.

When we apply this approach to sports — which is what we're here to do in these pages — it means that we seek the deepest possible explanation of fandom. In other words: Why are fans, fans? That underlying question started us down this path. While that journey began as a professional one, it has evolved into something personal: As lifelong fans ourselves, we knew fandom felt powerful, but we couldn't articulate why. Nor could we give up wrestling with that question.

That brings us back to the Camfields. Once you meet people like Nick and his dad, that question — Why are fans, fans? — takes on a remarkable weight. It's intellectually interesting, to be sure, but it's also emotionally compelling. The Camfields weren't the only people we met with emotive, compelling stories about their fandom. For Jennifer Klovee-Smith, another fan we interviewed, sports were a way to establish a steady connection with her father, despite his physical and emotional distance. Jennifer grew up in Olympia, Washington, with Mariners and Seahawks games providing the soundtrack for her childhood. When her parents divorced in the early 1980s, she was eight years old. Her father quickly remarried and moved to a horse farm, where Jennifer would visit him twice a month, on Sundays.

"He was always working," she recalled, "or he was inside watching sports." He wasn't the kind of guy who was going to ask Jennifer what was going on in her life, so she had to find a way to join him in his. "I remember sitting on the couch, and football was on, and no one was talking. I remember thinking, 'Okay, how am I going to get him to talk?'" So, she started asking questions: "What's a 'down'?" "When do they have to punt?" These questions got the conversation rolling, and both father and daughter leaned into it. "We watched every sport that was on: football, basketball, baseball," she told us. "I would ask questions about everything I could: positions, players, teams, the rules of the game. It didn't feel forced."

Even at that early age, Jennifer intuitively understood what sports could do for her family. Today, the connection between sports and her dad exists "on a subconscious level." Even though her dad isn't around all that often, when Jennifer watches a game with her own kids, she says, "I get to be connected with my dad in some way."

What would Jennifer's relationship with her dad be without sports? "It's hard to know, if I hadn't started asking all those questions, if we would have had that connection," she told us. A psychotherapist by profession, Jennifer understands both the power and the limitations of a parent-child relationship based solely on sports. On the one hand, she said, "I think it's sad that there weren't other things we could talk about." On the other, the fandom she shares with her father is invaluable, "because it's become such a big part of who I am. When people ask me what I got from my dad, I say I got my hair and my love of sports." She takes pride in being the mom who can talk sports with the dads at the school event, in being the mom who can toss a football with her son, in joining with her friends and her husband in this shared passion, and in passing the benefits of fandom down to their kids.

Whether it's between members of a close-knit, multigenerational family, or in a parent-child dyad held together by a single thread, people like Nick and Jennifer showed us that fandom adds depth to familial relationships. But that only scratches the surface of its power.

For Kyle Miles, a self-proclaimed "sports nut," fandom has paid enormous dividends. Kyle spent his formative years in Cape Town, South Africa, raised by a Scottish mom and a South African dad. "We're all sports mad," he confessed with gleam in his eye. His first sports loves — rugby, cricket, and soccer — reflect his ancestry. Those early interests solidified when he attended Stellenbosch University, a perennial sports powerhouse in South Africa's Western Cape province, where a rugby match between rival teams routinely draws upward of 25,000 fans. When Kyle immigrated to the US as a graduate student, on a scholarship to Kansas State University, he left his beloved sports behind. But his fandom traveled with him.

At K State, Kyle quickly immersed himself in the American college sports experience. His first basketball game happened to pit K State against their rivals, the University of Kansas Jayhawks. "When KU comes down the road from Lawrence to Manhattan, it's a really big game," he told us. K State won that night. The roaring crowd, the sweet victory, the human drama — this game started Kyle on a journey deep into American sports. Basketball, football, baseball: he now loves them all.

After graduating, Kyle landed in Kansas City, just in time to witness the Royals go to the World Series in back-to-back seasons and the Chiefs go to four consecutive AFC Championship games. This was an opportune time to broaden his love of sports and see his social network grow: "It was a natural layering on — as you're surrounded by these teams and fans and friends, you are going to games and barbecues. Those sorts of friendships laid the groundwork for feeling part of the fabric of what it means to be American."

Then Kyle started using sports to create similar opportunities for others.

Alongside the American sports he has adopted, Kyle has remained an engaged fan of his childhood favorites. A dedicated Liverpool supporter, he's been known to get up at 6 a.m. to tune into an English Premiere League game played halfway around the world. But watching a match alone is nothing like taking one in with a room full of fans. So, Kyle went on a hunt for local Liverpool fans. Through social media, he sent out-of-the-blue messages to anyone who appeared both to live in Kansas City and to love Liverpool Football Club, asking if they would be interested in watching a game at the Dubliner, a bar in the city's Power & Light District. Kyle estimates the first gathering garnered about fifteen fans. Today, thanks to the work of several core group members, they are an Official Liverpool Supporters Club, also known as the Kansas City Kop. A regular game brings one hundred fans to the Dubliner. And a big game? Upwards of six hundred fans spilling out into the plaza, watching on an enormous screen.

What does all this mean to Kyle? "It wasn't just the opportunity to get together and watch a game, because I can do that at home with some friends. For me it was about getting Kansas Citians together, wherever they're from. We have Irish, English, Aussies, people from India, other people from Africa. I met a Kenyan the other day. I get excitement and energy not just from having a large group of people together, but from engaging with people of different backgrounds."

For the Kansas City Kop, "It doesn't matter who you are, where you're from, your socioeconomic status, race, religion, you name it": If you share an interest in the Liverpool Football Club, you're welcome to join. "I didn't have that when I first came to Kansas City," Kyle told us. "I wish, from the day that I arrived, I could have found that camaraderie. I like helping put that together for other people."

Kyle didn't knowingly use fandom to build a new community when he moved to the US. But it's had that effect.

Other fans, like Brittani Johnson, a video game executive who grew up in the heart of football country, leverage fandom specifically to make new friends.

Brittani came to football fandom honestly. "You can't grow up in Texas and not experience Friday Night Lights," she told us. As a teenager, she participated in football in the ways girls could: as a cheerleader and a member of the school band's color guard. But her interests ran deeper than providing sideline entertainment. How deep? When it came time to apply for colleges, she considered schools based on their football teams' records. Ultimately, she enrolled at Texas Christian University, and her time there "ended up being the best four years of football for TCU. It was during the Andy Dalton time. If I think back to college, all my memories are about football."

As a student, Brittani had a work-study job recruiting for TCU's football team, as well as an internship with the NFL, preparing for the Super Bowl in Dallas. Both positions added gravitas to her football pedigree. By the time she graduated, Brittani had solidified her football bona fides. She could strike up a conversation about football with anyone, anywhere, anytime.

In 2009, she landed the role of Angel in the video game *Borderlands*. Then, in 2012, Brittani moved to Los Angeles to further pursue a career in the gaming industry. She now sees a direct correlation between her love of football and her success in a male-dominated field: "I did not go to school for the career that I have, but I was set up for success because I had the same interests as my colleagues. Football Sundays, even before I worked in video games, were dominant in my life. I'd rather have a meeting at a bar over a beer watching a game than in an office. So, being knowledgeable about sports has benefited me in my career. I wouldn't say it was intentional in the beginning, but I definitely caught on to the fact it was helping me."

Brittani serves as commissioner for her office fantasy football league. "I'm the only female in this league," she said. "The fact that I can coordinate these guys, that they lean on me to do that, that I'm able to talk about football as well as actually take part — they value that about me and gain a trust in me, and that opens them up for other conversations about life or work."

Brittani's fandom has also helped her make connections outside of work. On Sundays, in search of conversation and connections in her new city, she would walk to a restaurant called Sharkeez, in Hermosa Beach, and sit down at the bar. "I'd watch whatever game was on TV and literally talk to anyone who would walk up. Whenever I'm at a bar watching a game, I feel like I'm a little more open to meeting people. There's a little more air to me. I feel other people are like that, too. Whatever you're watching, it just opens you up to more conversation." One Sunday, a couple struck up a conversation with Brittani. Fast forward a few years, and now, "most of my friendships in LA can be traced back to that one interaction at Sharkees." Whether you're an immigrant from South Africa, or a migrant from Texas, fandom can help you find your place.

Like Britanni, Chris Falwell understands sports' function as a social superconductor. His story begins in Prince George's County, Maryland, a suburb of DC. There, he was brought up around people who loved sports. "My mom and dad were really competitive," he told us. "So, they put me in sports early on. My mom was a softball player, and my passion for baseball came from her. She was my Little League coach. She was out there driving me, teaching me. If a ball went between my legs, she'd be out there saying, 'Run that drill again,' putting me through it. I'd get frustrated, but I couldn't quit, because they did what parents do. They tell you, 'Pick your head up.' They say, 'It's gonna be okay.' They give you that confidence to practice, to perform, even when times are rough."

When unspeakable tragedy struck Chris's family, sports provided continuity. "My mom passed when I was nine. My dad passed when I was ten years old. But something I hold on to is their love and passion for sports."

Chris's maternal grandmother, who raised him after his parents passed away, maintained their legacy. "She made sure I made it to my games, she made sure I made it to practice. No matter what, she was always there. That's a vital part of life: There's nothing better than looking out into the stands and seeing a family member there. That was our quality time together."

Through high school, Chris's experiences as an athlete grounded him, and sports afforded him a connection to his grandmother and a circle of friends. But it wasn't until he moved to New York to start his career that he became aware of fandom's social power.

Chris was surprised to learn a quirk of the locals: They stick to their borough. "The guys I met and worked with in Brooklyn stayed in Brooklyn. They didn't go to the city. They were like, 'I'm gonna stay in my 'hood; I'm going to stay on my block.'" So, Chris would head into Manhattan alone, hoping to meet people. "I would go to a bar by myself, and if I tried to strike up a conversation with some guys, they would look at me like, 'Who's this weird guy talking to us?'" Chris persisted. And one day, that persistence paid off. He was sitting at a bar, watching a Knicks game, when he overheard some guys talking basketball. This was around the time of "Linsanity", Jeremy Lin's improbable run of success for the Knicks in 2012. "I jumped into their conversation and said, 'If he played for any other team, any other system, he would not be as good as he is.' The dudes thought I was crazy, but that moment opened the door. It wasn't, 'Who is this guy, why is he even talking to us?' We all had something in common: We were watching the game."

Enlivened by this interaction, he eagerly relayed the story to his girlfriend. "Well, when are you hanging out again?" she asked. But Chris explained it wasn't like that. "I didn't even know their names. There was no hanging out." It wasn't about those specific people; it was about a new understanding, a realization that he had a tool — sports — that could reliably help him create connections. "It became apparent how I best connect with people," he told us.

Having grown up as both an athlete and fan, talking sports was his sweet spot. "People would be surprised if I told them that I'm shy, but I am shy," Chris explained. Meeting new people, he felt awkward asking strangers questions like, "How are you?" or "What do you do for work?" But, then and now, when he talks about sports, "it comes off naturally. I speak with confidence. I speak like I know exactly what I'm talking about. So, I use sports to open up a conversation."

Now a banker living in San Diego, Chris continues to flex that social muscle every chance he gets. "Moving to California from New York, that's how I was able to connect with people. If you walk into my bank wearing a jersey, I want to talk to you about your team. Even if someone doesn't have the same passion I do, even if someone says, 'My grandmother bought me this stupid thing and I'm just wearing it as I walk around Walmart,' it's still a conversation starter."

One of those off-the-cuff conversations helped Chris find his footing in San Diego. "When I first moved out here, I saw this guy walking around in a Redskins[2] jersey. I said, 'Hail to the Redskins,' so he looked at me and said, 'Hail! Where are you from?' I said, 'PG County.' He said, 'I'm from Virginia. If you live out here, you should go to this Redskins bar.'" The following Sunday, Chris went down to Latitude 32 Pub & Grill. Even before he found the place, he heard the sounds of home: "They were blasting Go-Go music, which is a staple of DC. At first, I didn't really understand why I was hearing this music. I thought, this can't be coming from the same place I'm walking into." But it was. The minute he crossed the threshold into the bar, he was greeted with a "What's up, man? Welcome in." Since that day, Chris has had a place in San Diego where he can connect with his roots and find common ground with others.

Nick, Jen, Kyle, Britanni, Chris. Theirs are just a handful of the hundreds of stories we have encountered in our quest to understand fans. No matter whom we interviewed, no matter the sport or sports they were engaged in, no matter their social identities or personal histories, at the heart of their stories beat a constant theme: *To be a fan is to be part of a community.*

That statement — to be a fan is to be a part of a community — feels intuitively true. In fact, the social nature of fandom can feel so familiar and relatable that it's rendered nearly invisible. People tend to take it for granted, to accept it without really considering its implications. As lifelong fans, we were slow to recognize it ourselves.

Although we grew up in different places, surrounded by different teams, when we met, we quickly found that we spoke the common language of sports fandom.

David grew up outside of New York City during the 1980s, and he can't remember a time when he didn't follow sports. The Yankees were the starting point, quickly followed by the Jets, Knicks, St. John's basketball, and whatever else was on TV. He came of age around the time that sports radio became a thing, and WFAN encouraged him to have a take on everything. It was all he really did. He couldn't imagine a life lived any other way. Growing up, he was passionate, proud, always loyal to the team, with a dash of obnoxious New Yorker mixed in for good measure.

Ben grew up a world away: in Denver, Colorado, where the entire state revolves around the Broncos. Sure, the Nuggets were there when he was growing up, and the Rockies and Avalanche came to town as he came of age, but in Denver, it's all about the Broncos. He grew up during the reign of legendary quarterback John Elway, in a Bronco-loving family, where having an opinion on everything from who should start at linebacker to the offensive coordinator's play calling was ingrained in him. Like Dave, he was a passionate, proud fan, always loyal to the team (minus the dash of obnoxious New Yorker).

When we first started working together, we quickly bonded over our shared love of sports. As we deepened our investigation of fandom, we began to sense a tension between our assumptions about fans and the patterns we were seeing in our analysis of fan behavior. Our personal experience as fans was clouding our thinking. We thought we knew everything already because we spoke sports so fluently. It became clear to us that the language we use as fans — individually, collectively, culturally — is insufficient. We had to cut through this fog in order to successfully connect the dots.

And as we connected those dots, the true power of fandom became evident. If fandom is about community, then it should improve the social lives of sports fans. If fandom helps to improve the social lives of sports fans, then fans should reap the positive benefits of socializing. But what are the benefits of socializing? How far do those benefits extend? What is the potential of a phenomenon that brings people together in positive and meaningful ways, at the scale of sports? Could fandom — dare we say it — be a social good?

We had to find out. We pushed forward, asking questions, and then better questions, fielding surveys and then more surveys, uncovering new insights, interacting with more fans, and sharpening our hypotheses. What we discovered forever changed the way we think about and participate in fandom.

What if we told you that fans have more friends? Not only that, but what if we said that fans engage with those friends more often, and they value those friendships more? In fact, fans engage in and value their family relationships more, too. What if we told you that fans exhibit stronger measures of wellbeing, happiness, confidence, and optimism than non-fans? What if we told you that fans tend to be more trusting of others and more confident in institutions? Or that fandom helps mitigate the loneliness and polarization that plague our culture today?

Every time we have presented these findings — whether to renowned social scientists, to parents in the bleachers at a Little League game, or to a room full of sports industry insiders — we have received the same response: "That is not at all what I would expect."

We didn't expect it either.

Yet time and again, our analysis has led to unanticipated truths. Following one to the next, we arrived at a conclusion that, once seen, we could not unsee: Being a sports fan is good for you, good for others, and good for society.

We would not have written that sentence two years ago. Today, it is a motivating force in our lives.

A NOTE ON FOCUS

As our thinking about fandom crystalized, one thing became clear: When we talk about sports fandom, it's easy to focus on the wrong thing. In fact, there's a tendency to focus on peripheral issues, for better and for worse, that exist well outside the normal fan experience. For instance, critics will point out the obviously bad: boorish fans in the stands, violent hooligans fighting in the bar, post-victory mobs wreaking havoc on city streets. While this element certainly exists, it represents only a sliver of the fan population.

Make no mistake: we don't see fandom — or the sports industry as a whole — through rose-colored glasses. Violence and vitriol occur in every corner of our world. Greed and exploitation — of workers and consumers — exist in every industry. Of course, these widespread social ills will infect sports, too. We support the good work of analysts and social critics rooting out their causes and seeking solutions. But that's not our focus here.

We can also focus too heavily on sports' outsize positive effects. Advocates often point to historic moments in which sports galvanized Americans in moments of crisis. In a *New York Times* op-ed during the early days of the COVID-19 pandemic, Scott Boras wrote, "In some of America's darkest moments, the country has turned to Major League Baseball to bring hope and normalcy back to everyday life."[3] He cited incredible examples, ranging from President Franklin Roosevelt imploring MLB to continue to play after the attack on Pearl Harbor to Mike Piazza giving beleaguered New Yorkers hope by hitting an eighth-inning homerun for the Mets in the first game held in the city after the 9/11 attacks. Yes, these remarkable stories recount important, uplifting moments in sports. But when we rely on such historic outliers to prove the power of sports, we pull focus from the pervasive, positive impact of everyday sports fandom.

That is our goal here: not to get distracted by the outliers, positive or negative, but to highlight the normal, all-too-often overlooked behaviors of sports fans that, at scale, elevate the wellbeing — individually and collectively — of a large segment of the population.

To that end, this book blows past fan stereotypes and offers up a more meaningful — and more accurate — formulation of fandom. In the following pages, we will retrace the steps that led us to discover fandom's far-reaching benefits. Here, sports fans will find a new way of thinking about something undoubtably familiar, but too often misunderstood, undervalued, and trivialized. By the time you reach the final chapter, we trust that you, too, will see the power and potential that lies in one of the world's most universally shared passions. That is why we have spent the last two years distilling and contextualizing our journey in these pages: We want to help sports fans — and those who love us — understand the true impact of fandom, so they are inspired to live into their passion with purpose.

THE ROAD AHEAD
In this book, you will encounter a wide array of data, the results of myriad surveys and rigorous analysis. Through much trial and error, we have developed methods that accurately and consistently measure fan attitudes and behaviors. We have formed hypotheses, tested them, recalibrated, formulated new questions, and pressed ahead to gain ever greater insight, always testing, retesting, and pushing our thinking. We have uncovered patterns that reliably manifest over and over, in every context, without fail.

What unfolds across these chapters is, at least in part, a data story. In fact, the title, *Fans Have More Friends,* refers to one of the first data points we collected from our many surveys. That said, you do not need to be a data wonk to absorb — or enjoy — what we will present here.

About the graphics you'll see along the way: We feel it is essential for data geeks and non- to appreciate the consistency of the patterns we have identified. To that end, our charts lay bare phenomena that are steadfast, clear, and consistent. You don't need a PhD in statistics to understand them; just like fandom, they are accessible to all. We will walk you through the storyline that puts it all in context.

As much as the numbers matter, the data pales in comparison to the humans you'll meet along the way. While the data offers rigor and scale, the humans bring heart. They are real people who have become genuine friends, with us and with each other, due to the power of sports. They aren't just a static part of this book, but a dynamic part of our lives, participating with us regularly in fantasy football leagues and March Madness pools and post-game group-text analysis. For us, meeting these people has been the highlight of a journey that continues to this day.

Here's a roadmap for what's to come:

In Chapter 1, we break down common stereotypes and conceptions of fandom and provide a new framework for thinking about, talking about, and distinguishing between fans. This framework sets the stage for all the insights that follow.

In Chapter 2, we present our case that relationships — social interactions — are the driving force behind fan behavior. No matter how you look at it, the bigger a fan you are, the more friends you have.

In Chapter 3, we explore the dynamic relationship between fan activities and social engagement, which operates like a flywheel. We also demonstrate how those two components of the fan experience work together to improve personal wellbeing.

Chapter 4 focuses on a major threat to our wellness: loneliness. Here we argue that fandom, by increasing our sense of belonging, serves as a powerful antidote to loneliness.

Chapter 5 investigates another social ill: polarization. We explain how fandom — by bringing together people from different backgrounds — can shift our attitudes toward one another and the world.

In Chapter 6, we explore how social identity categories contribute to polarization, and how the "sports fan" identity can soften the hardened boundaries between "us" and "them," making more space for "we."

Finally, in Chapter 7, we encourage you to embrace the social power of your fandom, to deploy it to help heal an ailing world, and to teach others to do the same.

01   Reframing Fandom

Anyone who has spent four quarters in a football stadium, clocked nine innings in a ballpark, or gone tip-off to final buzzer at a basketball game has observed the full spectrum of fan types, from the "I'm here because I got free tickets" spectator to the die-hard, flag-waving, "I bleed team colors" fanatic. Nowhere have the opposite ends of this spectrum been more hilariously depicted than in the 1990s sitcom *Seinfeld*. If you've seen "The Face Painter" episode, which aired in 1995, you know where this is headed. If you haven't, hang tight. We've got you.

The scene begins with Julia Louis-Dreyfus's character, Elaine, sitting alone on her living room couch. She's waiting for her new boyfriend, David Puddy, who is offscreen, to get ready to go to the New Jersey Devils vs. New York Rangers Stanley Cup Playoff game.

"Hey, so how long have you been a Devils fan?" Elaine calls out.

"Since I was a kid," Puddy yells back. "I'm from Jersey."

"Yeah?" she says jokingly. "Well, we're going to kick your butts!"

"No way, man," Puddy's voice booms. "We're primed!" He sounds like he means it, and when he emerges from the back room — a tall, broad-shouldered man in a Devils jersey — Elaine sees that he does: He's painted onto his face a fire-red replica of the team logo.

Elaine does a classic *Seinfeld* doubletake: "What the— ?"

Puddy is oblivious to her shock. "So, what do ya think?" He's beaming with pride.

"What *is* that?" Elaine asks.

"I painted my face," he responds.

"You painted your face?"

"Yeah."

"*Why?*"

"Oh, you know," he responds: "Support the team."

"Well, you can't walk around like that," she tells him.

"Why not?" he asks.

"Because," she says, "it is insane."

"Hey — you got to let them know you're out there. It's the playoffs."

This exchange reveals the challenge inherent to investigating fandom: We don't know how to talk about it. The whys of fan behavior are explained in circular logic: Why do you dress up in team gear? Because you've got to support the team. Why have you got to support the team? Because — loyalty, man. Conversation over.

Worse, the face-painter stereotype, which dominates our collective imagination, depicts fandom as trivial, one-dimensional, and outrageous. Puddy's makeup is just the beginning. The next scene begins with the *Seinfeld* crew at the game. Elaine, Jerry, and Kramer sit in their rinkside seats, while Puddy stands, pounding on the glass. Later, out on the street, basking in his team's victory, Puddy erupts when a car stops just short of hitting him. He pounds on the hood and yells, "Hey, what are you doing?! Watch where you're driving, man!" He storms the passenger window, screaming at a priest seated on the other side of the glass: "Don't mess with the Devils, buddy. We're number one, we beat anybody! We're the Devils! The Devils!! Ahhhhhh!!!" Puddy runs away, leaving the priest shaken.

Of course, this iconic scene was exaggerated for comedic effect. But such images of fandom, ubiquitous in pop culture, influence our cultural conversation about fans. To reveal the depth and complexity of fandom, we need first to dismantle fan stereotypes.

Conventional conceptions of fandom run from the trivial to the toxic. On the trivial side, we have the man-cave dweller, surrounded by his sports memorabilia, his oversized TV, his logo-embossed leather couch, his beer fridge, and game-day chicken wings. Here, fandom is juvenile and fatuous. On the toxic side, we have the mob of post-championship fans drunk on victory, storming the streets, tearing down lamp posts, overturning cars, lighting fires, and picking fights with anyone wearing the other team's colors. Here, fandom is ominous and threatening, a conception embedded in the etymology itself. The word "fan" originated as an abbreviation of "fanatic," an adjective that originally used to describe possession by a god or demon. By association, the word "fan" conjures up images of boorish bros engaged in "possessed" and "insane" behaviors.

Of course, there's a degree of truth to this image, as anyone who's ever stood in a stadium restroom line can attest. Puddy feels familiar; we've all seen a Puddy in the wild. But as is the problem with all stereotypes, the "face-painter" limits our thinking. How can we argue that fandom has the power to activate social connections, mitigate loneliness, and soften polarization when the Puddy figure represents our common conception of fandom? How can something we believe to be so profound manifest in such a superficial — even pernicious — way?

Admittedly, fan stereotypes influenced our own perceptions when we started studying fandom as a phenomenon. Even as lifelong fans ourselves, we didn't truly understand what motivated fan behavior, nor did we appreciate its potential impact. But the more time we spent with fans, and the more critically we thought about fandom, the more we suspected that something powerful, something not yet named, loomed behind the "gotta support the team" logic. Slowly, as we observed fans in context, dug deeper into their motivations, and examined how fandom manifested in their day-to-day lives, a picture emerged that did not align with the Puddy-esque character.

It struck us not only that the stereotype was incomplete, but also that it masked the real power of sports fandom to make a positive, lasting impact. We found ourselves at an impasse. We had logically consistent qualitative insights that pointed us to a more elevated conception of fandom. But we needed quantitative survey data to see if these insights held up at scale. Testing our hypothesis through surveys required a reliable way to differentiate between fans. Differentiating between fans is a critical step because it enables comparisons between groups of people; such comparisons would illuminate the differences between less engaged and highly engaged fans, shining a light on fandom's true nature.

This required a more precise definition of fandom. Which meant that we needed to address a simple, yet critical question: What is a fan?

FAITH WITHOUT WORKS

At the beginning of this journey, conventional thinking, imprecise language, and rote assumptions stood between us and the core truths of fandom. To get where we wanted to go, we needed to break through these barriers and connect definitional behaviors with the lived realities of fans. In other words, we needed to break down fandom to first principles.

First-principles thinking is nothing new. It dates back to Aristotle, who defined first principles as "the first basis from which a thing is known."[4] Later, Rene Descartes picked up the idea up and ran with it, developing a method now called Cartesian Doubt, in which he systematically doubted everything he could until he was left with purely indisputable truths.

Namechecking Aristotle and Descartes sounds highfalutin, but what they describe is a relatively straightforward approach to problem solving: Remove assumption and convention until you are left only with what is essential. Applied to fandom, this means breaking down the fundamentals of the fan experience piece by piece, shedding the stereotypes, and then reassembling our conception of fandom from the ground up.

How do you identify the first principles of fan behavior? As strategists operating across the sports ecosystem for the past decade-plus, we have been tasked throughout our careers with solving a variety of fan-related business and brand problems. Along the way, we have been exposed to all sorts of fans, in all sorts of contexts. The benefit of this type of exposure is the ability to analyze, both broadly and deeply, fans and the factors that motivate them. Practically speaking, we spent countless hours interacting with and thinking about fans, asking ourselves questions like: What are the essential elements of fandom? A fan cannot be a fan without … what? Step by step, we cleared the mental detritus and began to identify the indisputable truths of fandom.

As we dug deeper, we noticed something strange: Conventionally speaking, the language we use to describe fandom is a function of self-proclaimed passion: *I'm a "huge" fan. She's "obsessed" with sports. That town is "rabid."* And yet, when it comes to sports, people claim "fandom," especially team-based fandom, even when they engage minimally, if at all, in fan behaviors. We're talking about the guy who considers himself a Fighting Irish "fan" just because his grandfather went to Notre Dame, or the woman who calls herself a Mariners "fan" simply because she lives in Seattle. Maybe they've attended a game or two; maybe they haven't. Maybe they own a team jersey; maybe they don't. Certainly, they can't name the current crop of key players, nor do they watch games regularly. They claim to *be* fans, but they don't *act like* fans. Even if they profess loyalty, they don't participate in the basic activities that characterize "true fandom."

Can you imagine the same thing happening with, say, music fandom? If you were to claim, "I'm a *huge* Rolling Stones fan," we'd presume that you engage in some key activities: For example, you own a few Rolling Stones albums, have a favorite song, have seen the Stones in concert. Maybe you have a "tongue and lips" poster in your garage. If you had or did none of those things, would you call yourself a fan? Of course not.

There's no question that passion is a fundamental component of the sports fan experience — more on this shortly — but, as the observation above makes clear, it's undeniably not the only component. More to the point, when it comes to understanding what makes fans tick, passion isn't a particularly useful organizing principle, mostly because it's a fundamentally subjective measure.

What is less subjective, however, is *action*. Sports fans seem intuitively to know this. Declare "I live for baseball" to a bunch of strangers, and they're likely to start peppering you with questions to qualify your statement: Who's your team? Who's your favorite player? How many ballparks have you visited? Ever been to spring training? As these questions suggest, passion is an ingredient, but it's not the only ingredient. Action must follow. True fandom requires both the emotional investment of *passion* and the temporal and financial investment of *action*. These are, to use Descartes's phrase, the "indisputable truths" of the fan experience and the building blocks of our conception of fandom.

COMMITMENT COMES WITH A PRICE

Guided by the principle that action is an essential ingredient of fandom, we set out to identify and measure a broad set of activities that fans engage in. We included common activities like watching sports on TV, as well as more niche activities, like betting

Activities that require attention

- Watch games at home — 89%
- Talk about games in person — 61%
- Watch games with friends — 49%
- Listen to sports radio — 45%
- Watch games at a sports bar — 37%
- Talk about games online — 33%
- Call into sports radio — 5%

Activities that require money

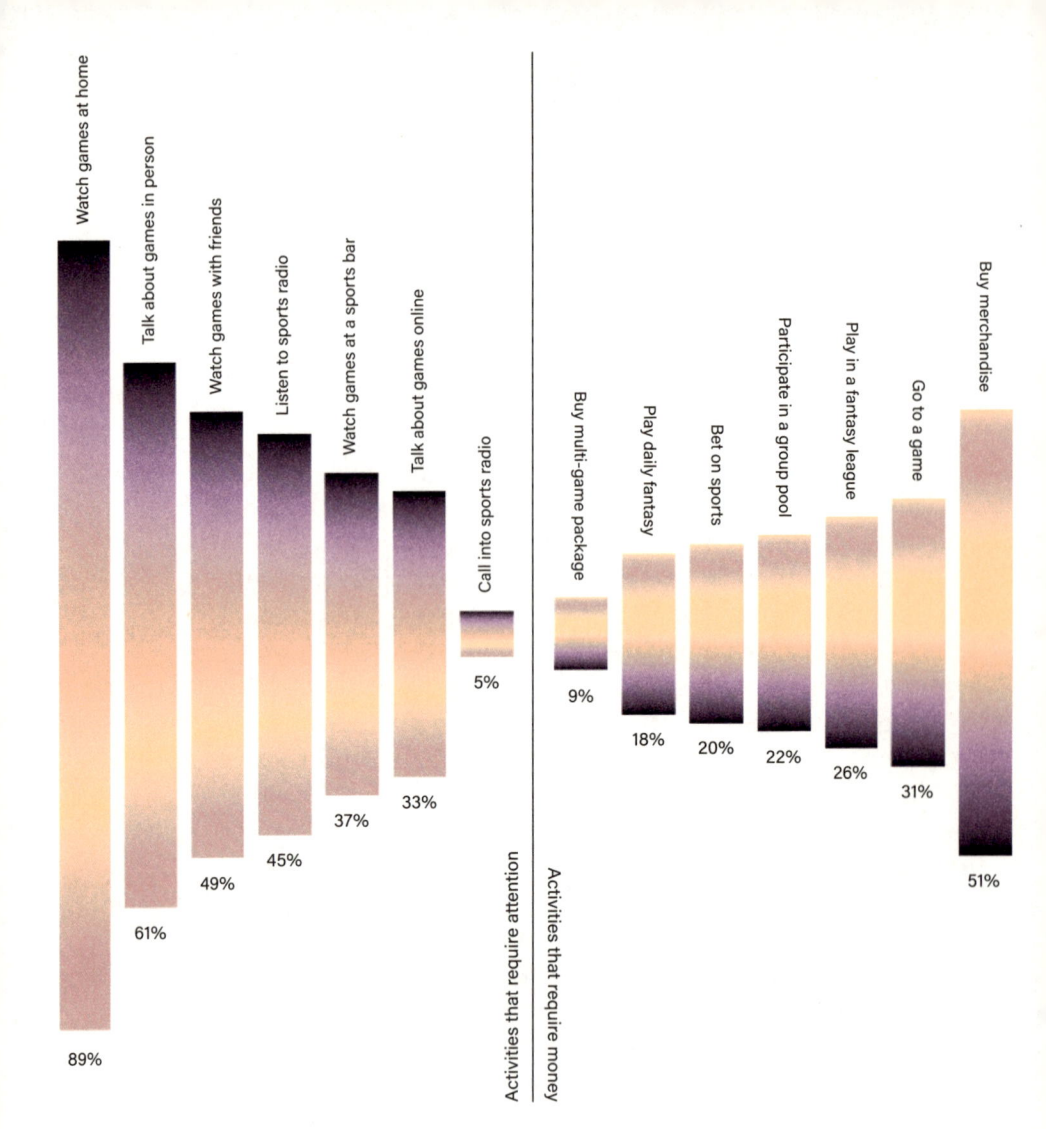

- Buy multi-game package — 9%
- Play daily fantasy — 18%
- Bet on sports — 20%
- Participate in a group pool — 22%
- Play in a fantasy league — 26%
- Go to a game — 31%
- Buy merchandise — 51%

1.1 **The percent of respondents who engage in each of these distinct fan activities.** N = 25,792. Q: Thinking of the last year, which of the following activities have you done in conjunction with the sports you follow?

REFRAMING FANDOM

on sports, playing daily fantasy, or calling into sports talk radio. We further separated these activities into two broad buckets: those that require *attention* and those that require *money*.

We have since surveyed more than 33,000 fans. The results shed light on the relationship between fan passion and fan action. Figure 1.1 shows the percentage of respondents who engaged in these various fan activities.

Fig. 1.1

As you can see, on the "attention" side, 89% of all fans watch sports at home, while only 5% call into sports talk radio. On the "money" side, 51% wear — and therefore presumably buy — team merchandise, while only 9% purchase multi-game ticket packages.

Interestingly, with the exceptions of watching and talking about sports, only a minority of fans (under 50% in most cases) engage in any of these activities. In fact, our surveys show that most self-proclaimed "passionate" fans engage in only a few fan activities. For example, nearly a third of self-proclaimed "passionate" NFL fans engage in only three or fewer activities commonly associated with passionate fans. So, just because your neighbor claims to be a "huge" fan, that doesn't mean that he's placing bets, playing in fantasy leagues, or regularly attending games. In fact, participation in these activities is surprisingly low. In other words, it's easy to say you're a fan, but it turns out that it's harder to act like a fan.

Clearly, not all fans who claim passion do the work we associate with fandom. On the other hand, as illustrated in Figure 1.2, of the NFL fans who do engage in multiple fan activities (between 7 and 14 of them), 84% rate themselves as passionate, as opposed to 71% of fans who engage in between 4 and 6 activities, and 48% of those who engage in 3 or fewer activities. So, we do see a positive relationship between passion and action.

Fig. 1.2

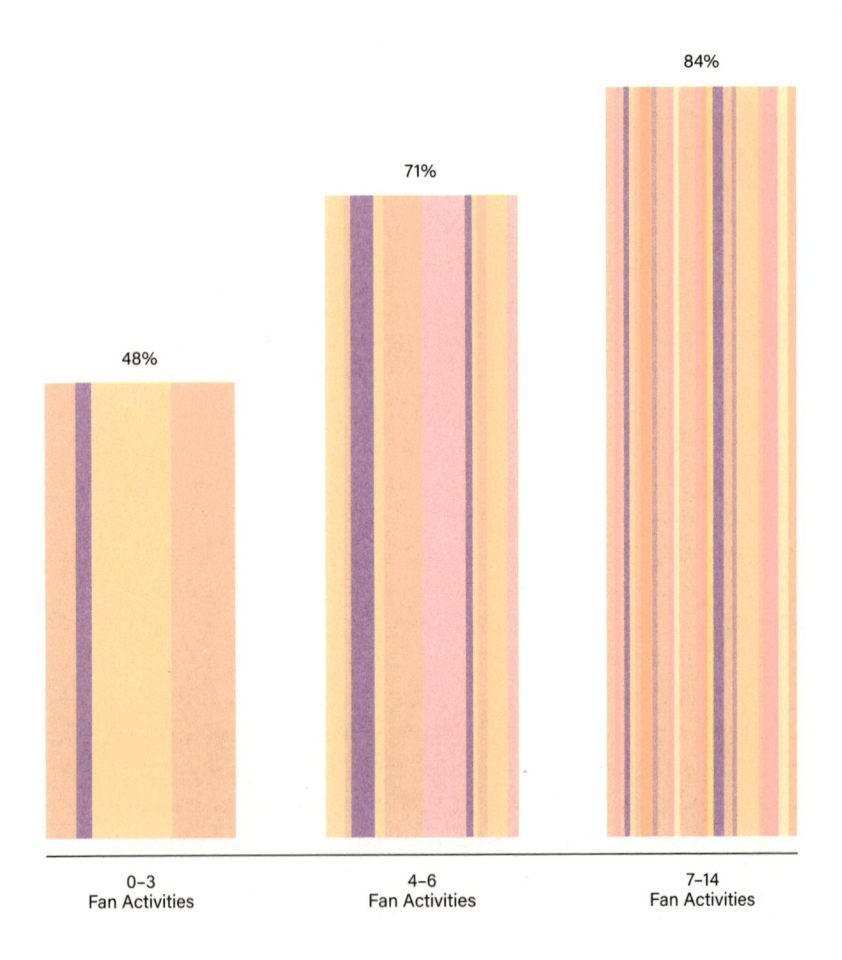

48% — 0–3 Fan Activities
71% — 4–6 Fan Activities
84% — 7–14 Fan Activities

1.2   **The percent who are passionate NFL fans at different fan activity levels.** N = 32,063.
Q1: Thinking of the last year, which of the following activities have you done in conjunction with the sports you follow?
Q2: How much of a fan are you of the NFL on a scale of 1 to 6, with 1 being "Not a fan of this Sport" and 6 being "Obsessed fan of this sport".

Fans who engage in more activities have higher passion scores. So far, so intuitive. In fact, as Figure 1.3 illustrates, we found that engaging in any single given fan activity correlates with a higher level of passion among NFL fans. It's worth noting that the more "niche" an activity, the higher the corresponding lift.

What we see here is consistent across our findings: Fans who engage in more actions report higher passion scores. For fans, action matters.

Fig 1.3

THE PASSION PROBLEM

We've established that action is one of fandom's indisputable truths. But we know that there's more to fandom than action alone. Passion does matter. But not all passion is created equal. Although we often assume that fan passion is one simple thing, in reality it manifests across multiple dimensions. This nuance is critical to sharpening our understanding of fandom. And without it, we would not be able to accurately differentiate between fans.

We discovered this insight through trial and error. The issue — as we would come to find out — was that we were struggling to reliably parse fan passion. We all know passion when we see it, but that doesn't make it measurable. The question is: How do you dimensionalize an elusive feeling in order to measure it?

Looking back, we encountered this problem many times over, but one example stands out: when we were conducting research for the New York Rangers.

We screened potential respondents using a variety of passion and action measures. All good. But once these "fans" entered the room, we immediately sensed the limits of their connection to the Rangers. They didn't talk or act like the diehard fans we saw at Madison Square Garden. When asked next-level questions about their engagement around the team, it became clear that these respondents were fans in the

Activities that require attention

Activities that require money

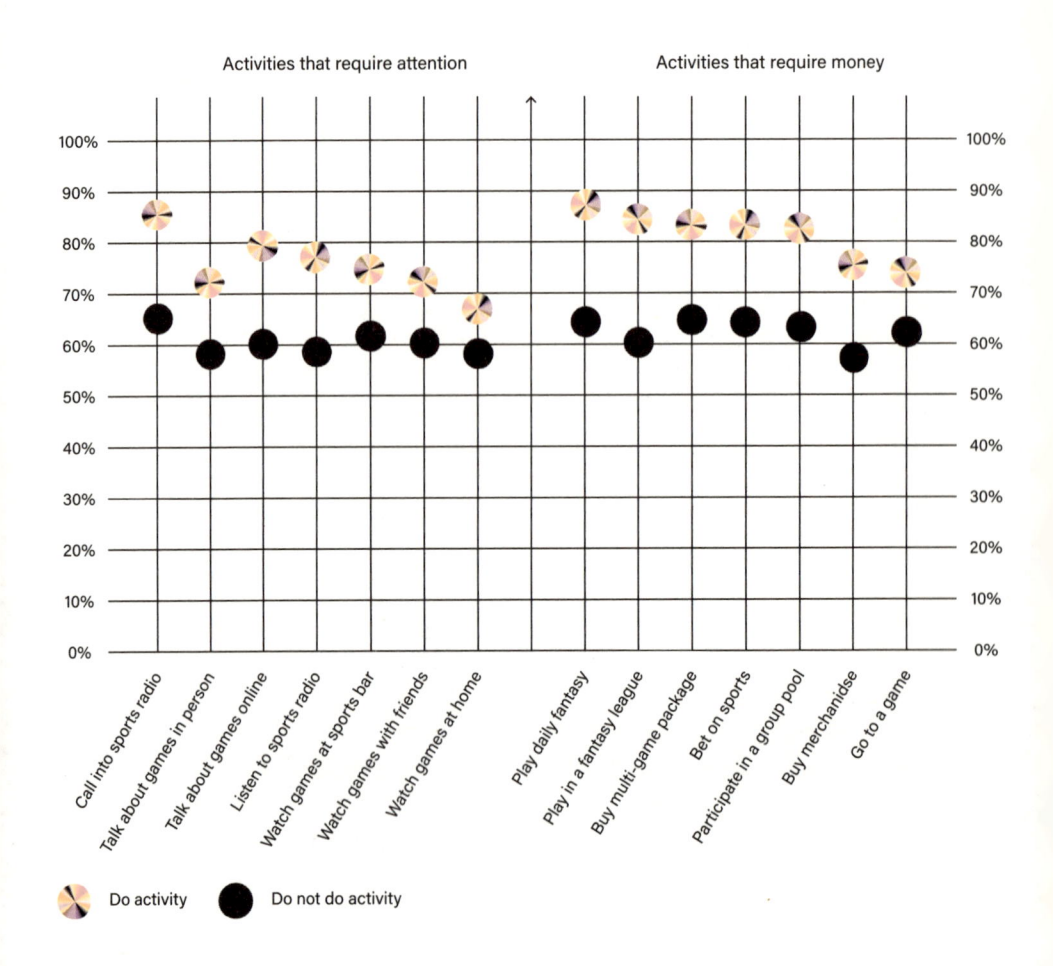

Activity	Do activity
Call into sports radio	~85%
Talk about games in person	~72%
Talk about games online	~80%
Listen to sports radio	~78%
Watch games at sports bar	—
Watch games with friends	~73%
Watch games at home	~67%
Play daily fantasy	~87%
Play in a fantasy league	~85%
Buy multi-game package	~85%
Bet on sports	~84%
Participate in a group pool	~83%
Buy merchandise	~75%
Go to a game	~74%

● Do activity ● Do not do activity

1.3 **The percent who are passionate NFL fans based on participation in individual activities.** N = 30,720.
Q: Thinking of the last year, which of the following activities have you done in conjunction with the sports you follow?
Q2: How much of a fan are you of the following sports? NFL – Scale 1 to 6, with 1 being "Not a fan of this sport" and 6 being "Obsessed fan of this sport".

most limited sense. Though they claimed Rangers passion and engaged in Rangers-related action, somehow, they did not reflect an abiding Rangers fandom.

Fortunately, not all was lost. As a point of contrast, we recruited a second focus group among Rangers season-ticket holders. When this group walked into the room, we knew they were fans even before they started talking hockey. The way they walked, the way they talked, their energy, their swagger — all of it made us feel like we were at The Garden. When they started talking hockey, they oozed authentic perspective. *Now*, we were talking to real Rangers fans.

In both instances, we recruited people with similar levels of action and self-reported passion, yet the two conversations yielded completely different results. Why? What were we missing?

Our experience with the Rangers revealed the problem, but we didn't uncover the solution until we explored college football fandom and daytime sports talk show viewership, respectively.

ENGAGEMENT WITHIN A SPORT

When we first set out to understand college football fandom, we assumed that fans who had gone to a "football" school like Alabama, USC, or Notre Dame would have a qualitatively different relationship to college football than fans who had not gone to such a school. These fans, we figured, don't simply graduate with a degree; they graduate with *a team*. Using this team lens, we segmented our various focus groups by alumni of schools with major college football programs and non-alumni (that is, college football fans who did not attend a school with a major football program).

We did see a contrast between these groups — just not in the way that we expected. As it turned out, the non-alumni fans exuded a love of college football that most of the alumni seemed to lack. Further, that passion translated into significantly more action.

Simply put, the non-alumni were more engaged college football fans.

When alums of football schools talked about their fandom, they told crazy "I was there when" stories. They described taking annual pilgrimages back to campus, or organizing watch parties for alumni groups in their towns. They never missed one of their alma maters' games. But, their fandom generally centered on one team.

Non-alumni fans, on the other hand, followed college football more broadly. Sure, they had favorite teams and strong rooting interests, but they dedicated their Saturdays to watching any game on TV. Some ran college football pools, while others could give you informed takes on any team in the Power Five conferences and beyond. These people immersed themselves in the joyous feeling of college football Saturdays: the campus traditions, the marching bands, the student sections, the whole shebang.

If the non-alumni fans shredded our initial hypothesis — that "football school" alumni would be bigger fans than non-alums — they also led us to a greater insight: Fandom is stickier when fans have an orientation *to the sport*, not just *to a team*. These two modes are not mutually exclusive: A single fan can love college football generally and root for the Crimson Tide specifically. But when they do both, their fandom runs deeper. Why? First, if your interest is not strictly team-oriented, you are likely to watch more games. Second, the ebbs and flows of your team's fortunes will have less impact on your overall interest, so even if your team is having a bad season, you have other reasons to engage. Third, and perhaps most importantly, you have more opportunities to share your fandom. Think about it: A fan who follows the entire college football landscape has a lot more to discuss at a neighborhood barbecue than does someone who can talk only about USC.

We tested this new hypothesis on the other five of the Big Six American sports leagues (namely, the NFL, MLB, college football, NBA, NHL, and college basketball). We created a question to understand a given fan's passion orientation: Will you watch this sport no matter who is playing or only if your team is playing? As you'll see in Figure 1.4, fans oriented toward the sport are dramatically more passionate than those oriented toward a team. For example, among college football fans, 49% of fans who watch only if their team is playing consider themselves to be "passionate" and 74% of fans who watch no matter who is playing report themselves as "passionate." In fact, "league-oriented" fans outrank "team-oriented" fans by at least 20% in terms of passion across the Big Six.

To be clear, league-oriented fans can also be dedicated supporters of a team, but league orientation signals increased levels of fan passion.

This nuanced understanding of fan passion adds a critical dimension to our understanding of the fan experience. When we look back at what we missed in those initial Rangers focus groups, we now see that the less engaged group had an affinity *for the team* but had no real tie *to the sport*. In contrast, the highly engaged group had an almost spiritual connection with the game of hockey. They lived the values of hockey. Some played the game, some had kids who played. They all loved the game and the NHL as well as the Rangers. This insight brought us one step closer, but the full picture of fandom still wasn't quite complete.

ENGAGEMENT ACROSS SPORTS

We found another dimension of fan passion when we were trying to understand viewership of daytime sports talk television programs. From the outset, we knew that anyone who spent considerable time watching daytime sports talk programming — think

Fig. 1.4

	NFL (n = 21,899)	MLB (n = 16,586)	NBA (n = 14,434)
	58%	50%	38%
	84%	76%	75%

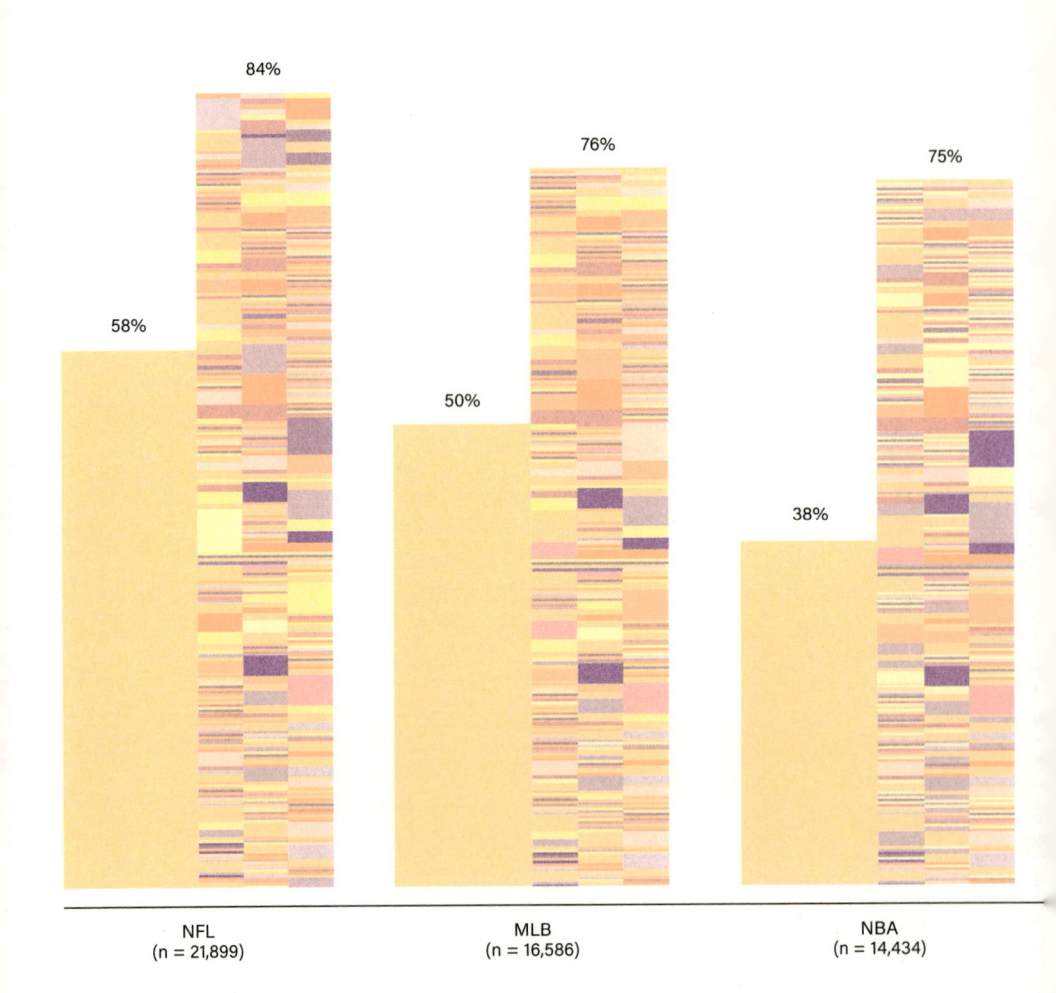

                74%
                                67%
                                                64%
        49%
                    40%
                                    38%

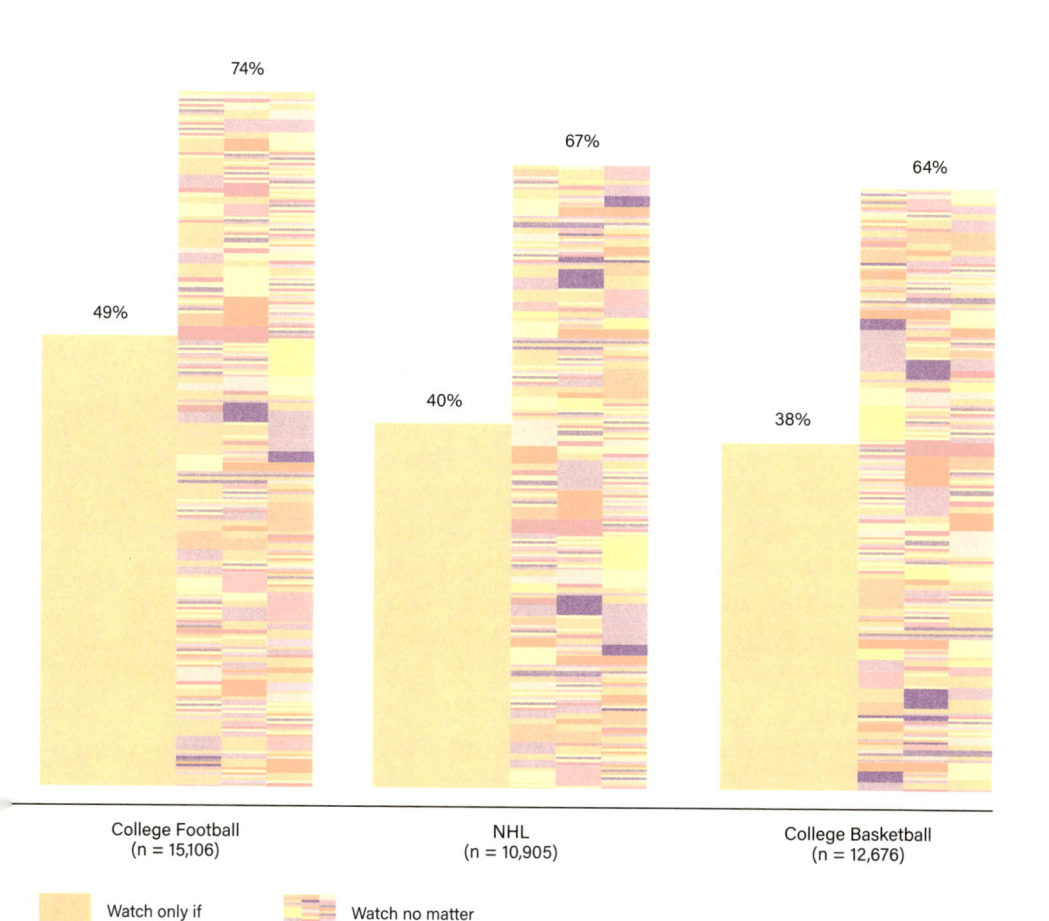

College Football   NHL   College Basketball
 (n = 15,106)   (n = 10,905)   (n = 12,676)

▢ Watch only if   ▦ Watch no matter
   my team is playing   who is playing

1.4 **The percent who are passionate fans of the sport based on whether they "watch only if their team is playing" versus "watch no matter who is playing".**
Q1: How much of a fan are you of the following sports?
Q2: Which of these statements comes closest to how you typically engage with each sport: "I'll watch any game no matter who is playing" or "Typically only watch games if my team is playing"?

51

Fox Sports' *Skip and Shannon: Undisputed* or *The Herd with Colin Cowherd*, or ESPN's *First Take* and *Pardon the Interruption* — was likely a dedicated fan. The usual docket of games on weekends and weekdays is not enough to satiate these fans' sports appetite: They want more. As we spent more time with this audience, it became clear that these fans engaged with sports in ways that were both broad and deep. They followed leagues and players as much as teams. And, most importantly, their fandom extended across multiple sports.

For example, a multi-sport fan might be a San Francisco 49ers season-ticket holder, but she also has a subscription to NBA League Pass and roots for whomever LeBron James is playing for. Another fan might love the Atlanta Hawks, but he also watches Sunday Night Football every week. "Sports fan" — emphasis on the plural — is a key part of their identity, a moniker that complements their multi-team and multi-league fandom. These folks pride themselves on having nuanced opinions on topics as varied as MJ's GOAT status, the legitimacy of the DH, and the merits of the Cover 2. They regularly consume shows that discuss a variety of topics across sports, and that rarely, if ever, touch on their favorite teams (unless they're lucky enough to be a Dallas Cowboys fan). To restrict their fandom to a specific team or sport would be like removing a section of their brain.

This cross-sport fandom signals elevated levels of engagement. This idea makes intuitive sense. Just think about the avid Chicago Bears fan who has owned season tickets for two decades. He lives and breathes the Bears and hasn't missed a home game in years. Despite his obvious passion, his fandom is limited to a single season. Sure, he's following Bears news all year long, but he's locked in for only a handful of months. Compare his seasonal fandom to a Chicago sports fan who follows not only the Bears but also the Bulls, Cubs, and Blackhawks, too. Her fandom is multi-sport, extending her engagement year-round.

The bottom line is that engaging across multiple sports results in a stronger attachment to each individual sport. In fact, we can predict your NFL fandom — or that of any other Big Six sport — based on the number of other sports you follow. Figure 1.5 shows how a fan's passion for the NFL grows in direct relationship to how many other Big Six sports they engage with passionately.

Fig. 1.5

On the far left, 38% of respondents who are not fans of any of the other Big Six sports rate themselves as "passionate" about the NFL. The fact that they are not passionate fans of any other sports signals lower levels of passion for the NFL. This is our Chicago Bears season ticket holder from above. If you move toward the right, adding just one additional sport, the passion rating for the NFL jumps to 67%. This increase continues incrementally with each additional sport, until we get to the far right side of the chart: if you are passionate about all of the other five of the Big Six sports, then there's a 99% chance you're also a passionate NFL fan.

This phenomenon is not unique to the NFL. The pattern holds for all sports. Why? The simple answer is that a multi-sport fan doesn't have an offseason, which means they remain in fan mode all year long. In other words, they get more reps. The repetition and reliability of their fan activity engrains fandom more deeply into their everyday lives. The more their fandom is reinforced by participating in these activities, the more they identify with it. The more they identify with it, the more they engage in it. And the more they engage in it, the more profound their fandom becomes. It's a virtuous cycle.

A second reason multi-sport fans engage more deeply is that they have a variety of different fan experiences across these different sports. Each sport

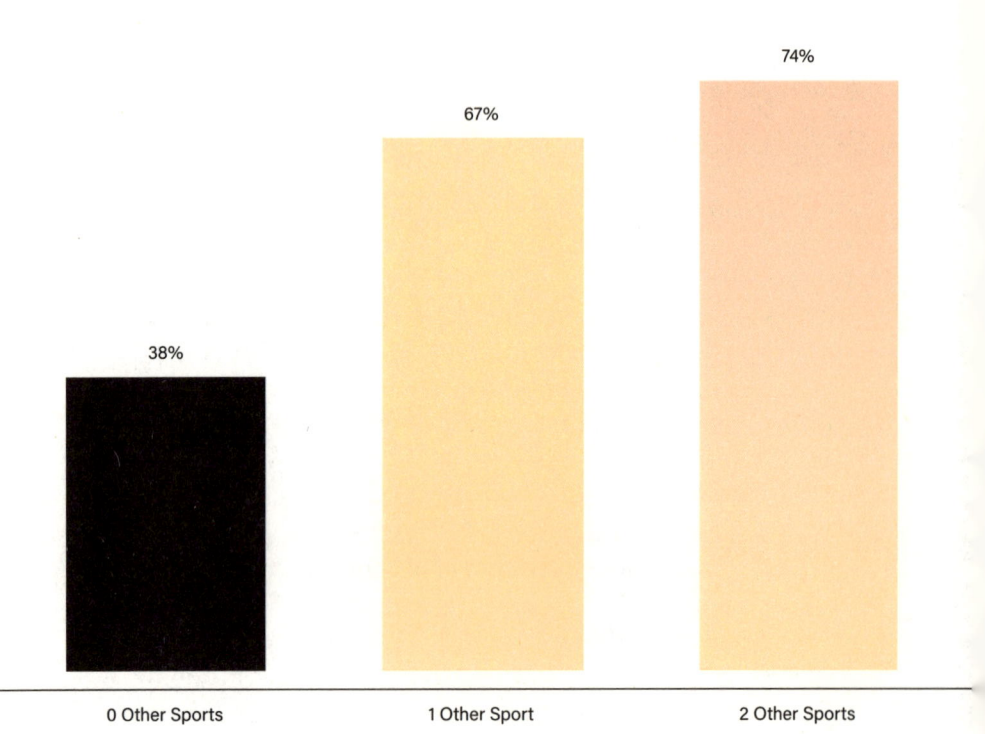

	38%	67%	74%
	0 Other Sports	1 Other Sport	2 Other Sports

                                                        99%
                                    95%
                88%

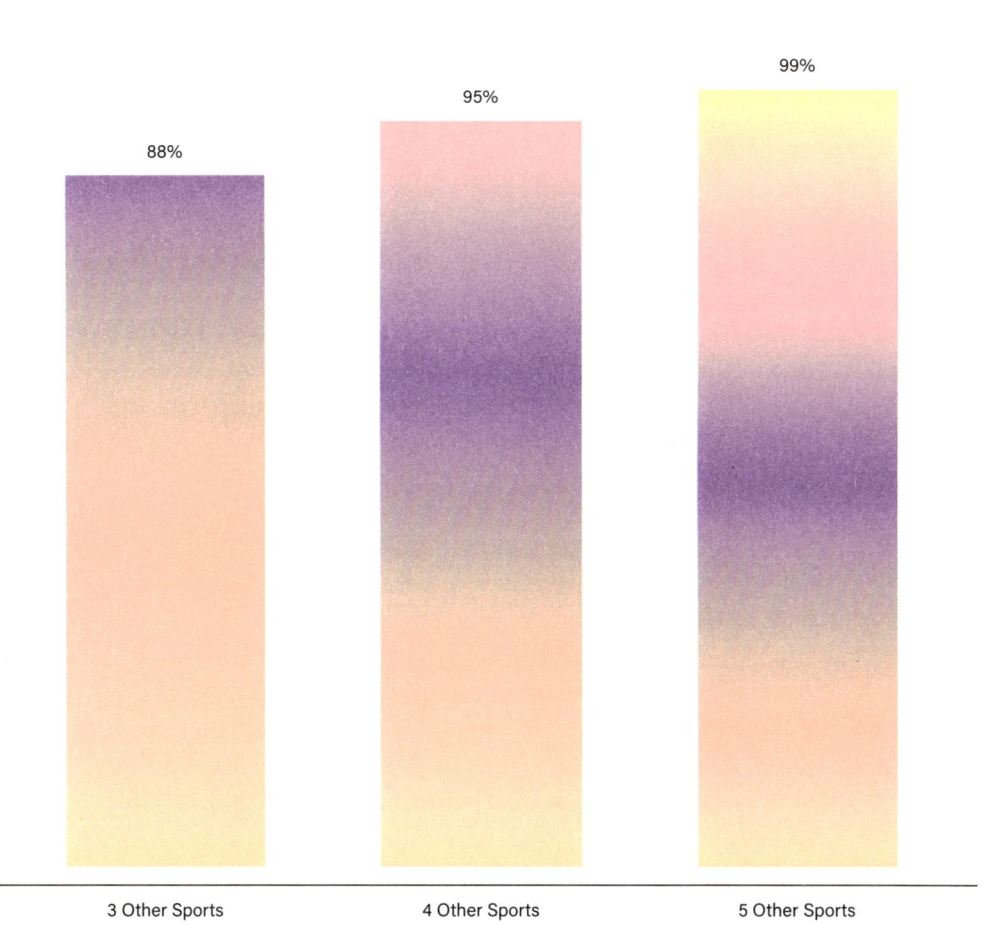

         3 Other Sports   4 Other Sports   5 Other Sports

1.5   **The percent who are passionate NFL fans based on the number of other sports they are a passionate fan of.** N = 32,063.
        Q: How much of a fan are you of the following sports? The big 6 sports here are the NFL, MLB, NHL, NBA, College Football, and College Basketball.

has its own rhythms, rituals, and histories; each offers unique fan traditions; and fans develop unique connections to each. For example, you may have a different origin story for your baseball fandom than you do for your college football fandom. This variety naturally gives you greater perspective, context, and appreciation for the particulars of all the sports that you follow.

The third and most important reason multi-sport fans tend to be more engaged fans is that the social network around each of those sports is likely to be different. Our Bears season ticket holder from the example above likely has a robust set of people in his life with whom he shares his Bears fandom. But the fan of all the Chicago teams likely has an active social network for *each* of those teams. Sure, there's bound to be some overlap between those groups, but each team will add new people to her orbit.

Again, looking back at what we missed in those Rangers focus groups, we now see that the less engaged group did not express elevated interest in any of the other major sports. On the other hand, the highly engaged group had similar hot takes about the Knicks, Yankees, Giants, Jets, and Mets. These takes revealed an authentic passion for all of these sports; they were New York fans in a holistic sense. Adding this dimension of fan passion completed our picture of fandom.

THE FAN VALUE SCORE

So, where is our conception of fandom now? We have the two building blocks of fandom: passion and action. We also have two ways of adding dimension to that passion: breadth within a sport and breadth across sports. These are the first principles of the fan experience, fandom's indisputable truths. Most importantly, these fundamentals give us measurable actions and attitudes that we can use to differentiate between fans, from the unengaged to the highly engaged. Armed with that ability, we can now identify the most dedicated fans and investigate what motivates their behavior.

To that end, we created a new tool: the Fan Value Score. This tool measures action, passion, and league orientation, and accounts for multiple sports. It assigns point values to each element and places the fan on a continuum from a minimum score of zero to a maximum score of fifty-three, which we subsequently separated into more readable tiers called Low-Value, Mid-Value, and High-Value. As you will see in the following pages, we also typically include a group called Non-Fans.

In both theory and practice, developing a tool like the Fan Value Score requires a blend of art and science.[5] Since we locked in on this approach in the fall of 2019, we have run dozens of surveys, reaching fans and non-fans alike, to probe various aspects of their attitudes, behaviors, and personalities. In all these surveys, we've asked the same Value Score questions to more than 25,000 people.

Ultimately, our goal was to depict fandom faithfully so we could identify the most engaged fans and uncover actionable insights into their motivations. Now, with stereotypes dismantled and a new, more accurate picture of fandom built up in their place, we could get down to the business of understanding the differences between fans. That pursuit would take us from focus groups to stadiums, living rooms, sports bars, barbershops, and backyard barbeques. At some point along the way, we realized we were not simply gaining relevant insights to benefit the sports industry. As our country spiraled into an era marked by pandemic-induced isolation, social unrest, and political division, we were learning about the power of fandom to positively impact people's lives.

02 Fans Have More Friends

"If you're born in New York, you're born a Knicks fan. It's just instilled in you."

So declares Greg Armstrong. Yes, Greg was born in the Bronx, in 1964, the youngest of three siblings. But if you ask him when he became a fan, he won't give you his birthdate. Instead, he'll tell you about his family. "My brother was four years older than me, and I looked up to him," he told us. "We shared a room, and he was a big Knicks fan, so we had posters all over the walls. We watched all the games together on Channel 9, then we would go outside and play basketball in the schoolyard together. It was a bonding experience for us."

Greg's childhood was a fortuitous time to become a Knicks fan: It was the era of Walt Frazier, Willis Reed, and Earl Monroe. Around the time of the run-up to the team's second championship season in 1972–73, Greg's mom gave him a pair of Knicks pajamas. "I just kind of took it from there," he says, talking to us from a home office decorated floor-to-ceiling with Knicks' memorabilia. Though that championship marked a pinnacle the Knicks have not reached since, Greg's fandom has never waned. "They just became a passion. I would watch every game on TV and root hard for the team."

In high school, Greg got his first taste of Madison Square Garden. "We used our student GO Card and would buy six-dollar tickets, all the way up in the blue seats," he says, referring to The Garden's upper deck. That was in the early 1980s, and at that time the Knicks weren't very popular, so Greg and his friends would sneak into the better sections of the half-empty arena. "The ushers, they didn't really care. They didn't really give you a hard time, I guess, because most of the seats were empty." As he recounts these memories, Greg radiates the impishness of a teenager who copped lower-level seats for the cost of a bootleg cassette tape.

During that run in the 1980s, the Knicks never advanced past the Eastern Conference Semifinals, but a diehard fan like Greg remained loyal. In 1991, the Knicks announced Pat Riley as the new head coach, and Greg sensed change on the horizon. "That was it. I said, 'Pat Riley is coming to New York. We got to be there.'" By then, Greg was married, managing a grocery store, and raising kids in Yonkers. "I didn't even know if I could afford season tickets," he says. "I wanted to take my kids to the games — they were toddlers at the time — and try to bring them up in the fandom. I wanted to share my passion, to pass it down to them. So, I called Madison Square Garden and they had a location that was suitable for my budget. It was an expense, but I was able to squeeze it in." In his first year as a season ticket holder, he paid $24 a ticket.

Greg's instincts were right: The tide turned. For the next decade, the Knicks reached the post-season every year, including two NBA Finals appearances, in 1994 and 1999. Then everything fell apart, except for Greg's fandom. By the time we met him, in 2016, at an informal focus group with Knicks season-ticket holders, Greg had been a season-ticket holder for 25 years. All in, Greg has invested a considerable amount of money into his fandom. In addition to the tickets themselves, which we can assure you cost more than $24 per seat today, he regularly shells out money for gas — commuting an hour upstate each way — bridge tolls, and parking just to get to the games. That's on top of the substantial time investment required to attend more than 30 home games a season for 30 seasons. Despite those costs, you can usually find Greg in his seats, win or lose. And for the last 20 years, the Knicks have done a lot of losing.

What motivates a fan like Greg to buy season tickets year after year, just to watch a disappointing team? As he tells it, "When they started losing, initially, you think that it's just going to come back.

You're thinking that this is a blip. We're going to be good again. So, for one, two years, it is not really a big deal. But then, as it keeps going on, it gets a little tough. The good times that you had keep you hoping, even though the team is terrible. Your passion takes over — you love this team, you love this sport, you know they'll get good again eventually, and you want to be there when it happens. You don't want to turn your back on something that you have invested so much time and energy into. For me, it was a no-brainer: I love the Knicks. That's something that I grew up with. I couldn't leave."

Greg is speaking in fan vernacular here — passion, loyalty, dedication, hope — all of which we, as fans, understand viscerally. But as strategists tasked with uncovering consumer motivations, when we tapped on his fan language, it sounded hollow, like a false wall hiding a secret room. What's behind it? Why spend an inordinate amount of time and such a large percentage of your disposable income to watch twenty years of, in Greg's own words, "terrible, terrible basketball"?

WHY WOULD YOU DO THAT?

In boardrooms, academic circles, and barrooms alike, we have encountered many theories about fan behavior. Some believe that sports offer compelling entertainment or an escape from the real world. Others say that fandom helps people establish their personal identities. Still others argue that sports allow fans to feel connected to something larger than themselves. Like Greg's explanations of loyalty, passion, and hope, there's a measure of truth to all of these theories. But — for us, at least — none adequately explain why the Gregs of the world do what they do. Either they're crazy, or there's a rational explanation for such devotion. We were determined to find that rational explanation.

To find it, we needed to look at fans more holistically, exploring their activities within the broader contexts of their lives, always asking ourselves: What "job" is their fandom doing for them?

When we met Greg, we were focused on uncovering the "job" Knicks fandom does for Knicks fans — and, by extension, the function that intense fandom performs for supporters of any team. To get at the answer, we conducted ethnographic research that took place in three parts. First, we went to the fan's home, meeting family, pets, and even neighbors, and inevitably touring massive memorabilia collections. Second, we attended a game with each fan to see firsthand how they experienced their team. Finally, we tagged along with the fan on an activity that had personal significance to that person; this was an open-ended exercise that added dimension to the fan's story. After our initial meeting with Greg, we called him up to see if he'd like to participate. He, along with seventeen other fans, jumped at the chance.

With his megawatt smile and friendly manner, Greg is a good hang and a gracious host. At his home in Middletown, NY, he regaled us with stories sparked by his museum-worthy collection of Knicks swag. He revealed that while the Knicks are his true love, he's obsessed with the NBA in general, and is also a dedicated fan of the New York Yankees and the New York Giants.

While our home visit was entertaining, it wasn't until we walked into The Garden with Greg that we started to see the underpinnings of his fandom in action. Here, he was in his element. He wasn't in the building more than five minutes before everyone from ushers to fellow fans were waving him over for a chat. When we finally reached his seats, we saw how deep these Garden friendships ran.

As we were getting settled in, Greg and his season-ticket neighbor greeted each other warmly and seamlessly slipped into a conversation without skipping a beat. The comfort and intimacy they demonstrated was notable. Later, Greg told us, "It's not just about going to the game and rooting on the team ... the lawyer who sits next to me — he's been here sitting next to me for all twenty-five years I've had the tickets. I watched his kids grow up and he watched my kids grow up. We've become good friends. The different people who sit around you in the section — they become almost like your extended family." Greg was quick to say hi to fans and Garden staff in the neighboring sections, too, greeting them by name. All in all, we could see what he meant when he said, "I'm at home at The Garden."

This experience was top of mind when we accompanied Greg to his barbershop, Fuzion in Middletown, NY, for the last part of our research. He chose this spot because it's a place where his fan persona thrives. Importantly, it's a place where the social currency he has accumulated via his lifelong Knicks fandom pays off. The minute he walked through the barbershop door, his mere presence shifted the conversation to the Knicks among barbers and clients alike: commiserating over losses, sharing stories from the glory days, offering hopeful predictions for the future. All the while, we noticed that other topics came up, too: kids, jobs, promotions, marriages, births, deaths, disappointments, etc. The Knicks anchored a conversation that eventually provided the space for friends old and new to catch up on life beyond basketball. And Greg was at the center of it all, reveling in the sense of community that his Knicks fandom created.

One might assume Greg's personality accounts for all these friendships. After all, he's an affable guy, likeable, and as eager to listen as he is to talk. But these interactions — the season-ticket neighbors, the back-and-forth with ushers, the barbershop reminiscences — were common among all the fans who participated in our research. As we chronicled their lives, we began to see these social connections as the real incentive motivating the most engaged fans. In other words, *this was the "job" their fandom performs.* Suddenly, Greg's decision to invest so much money and time to watch bad basketball no longer seemed irrational. As we started to look at the season-ticket value proposition this way, the math changed. Despite what he might say about team loyalty, the team was not the primary factor in his purchase decision. What he was buying — what he is buying to this day — is *belonging.* As it turns out, the real reason to be a fan is to be a part of a community.

A TESTABLE HYPOTHESIS

Since convening that research with Greg and his fellow Knicks season-ticket holders, we have surveyed tens of thousands of people, interviewed hundreds of fans, and spent innumerable hours in barrooms and stadiums around the country, in search of a unifying theory of fandom. At each stop, we refined our approach, gathered more data, and analyzed it from new perspectives. Again and again, we found ourselves heading in the same direction. We sensed we were approaching an insight that could dramatically shift our collective understanding of fandom. But we needed to bring the idea into focus, flesh out the thinking, and develop a method to test our hypothesis.

We had arrived at our "to be a fan is to be part of a community" theory, based on a compendium of emotionally rich, revelatory stories like Greg's. But could we demonstrate that insight at scale? If we could do so once, would the results hold up over time? As a first step, we set out to test a more precise hypothesis: If social interactions animate fandom, then more engaged, higher-value fans should have a more robust social life. Or, more plainly: *The bigger a fan you are, the more friends you will have.*

As it turns out, counting friendships is more complicated than it seems. Try it: how many friends do you have? It's a difficult question to answer, because our brains don't work that way. We need to categorize before we can count. To get reliable responses, we needed an organizing principle simple enough to help people access their answers, but complex enough to produce useful data. Our solution was to categorize friendships into common origin points — childhood, high school, college, work, kids, fitness activities, and so on — and then ask respondents about the friends they met through those origin points.

For each relevant friendship origin point, we asked three simple questions: (1) How many friends do you have from this origin point? (2) How much do you value those friendships? (3) How often do you interact with those friends? Apart from producing a reliable total number of friends, these questions added dimension to each respondent's social network. They also sharpened our hypothesis: if High-Value Fans are motivated by social experiences, then High-Value Fans should not only have more friends, but they should value those relationships more, and engage with those people more often.

We have asked this same battery of questions to more than 30,000 people in 11 surveys since January 2020. We then segmented survey respondents into four groups based on their Fan Value Score: Non-Fans, Low-Value Fans, Mid-Value Fans, and High-Value Fans.

The results? Fans do, in fact, have more friends than non-fans. What's more, they value those relationships more, and engage with those people more often. Engagement amplifies this effect, too: not only do fans have more friends than non-fans, but High-Value Fans have more friends than Low-Value Fans.

Fig. 2.1

Let's take a closer look at the results. Figure 2.1 captures the average number of friends for each

	35.6

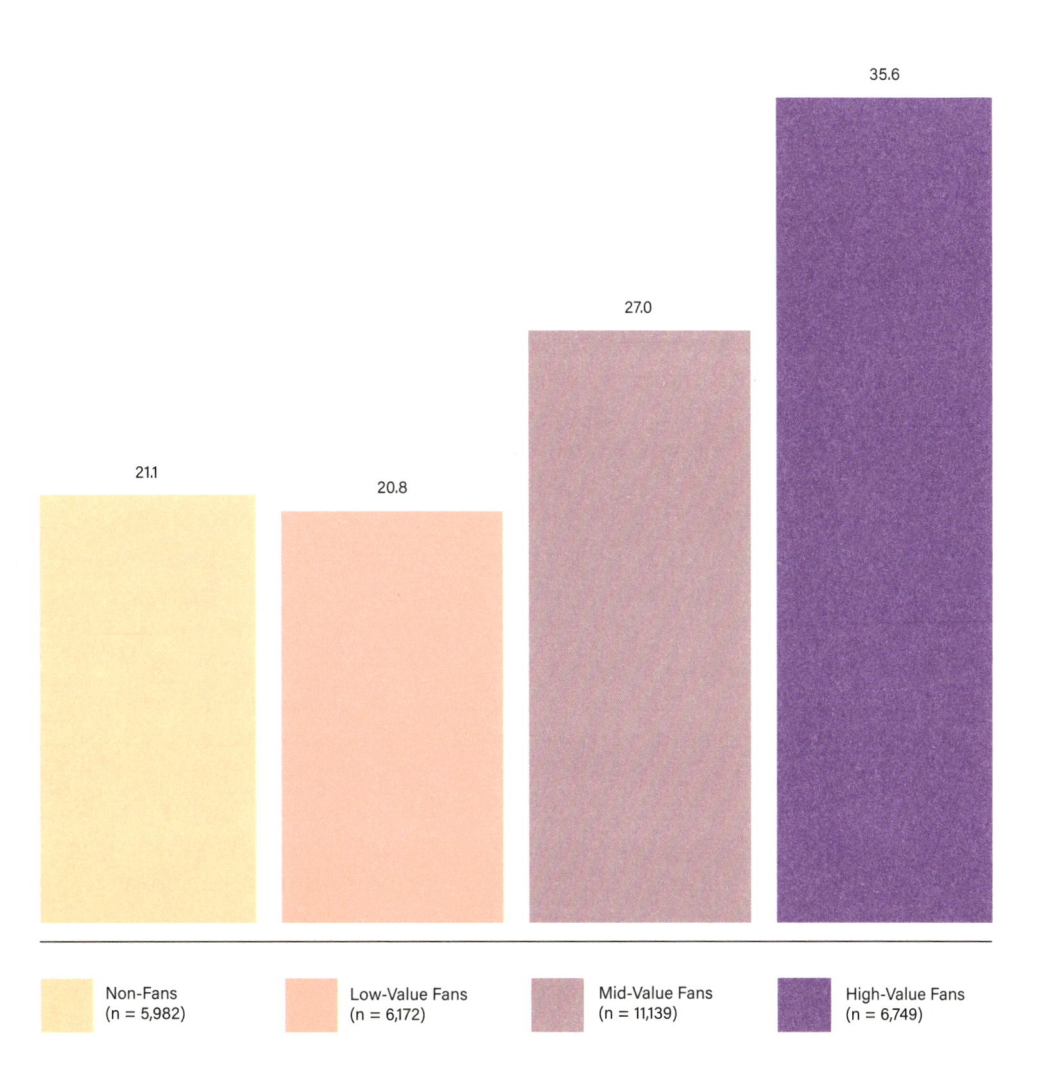

                                                    27.0

    21.1   20.8

Non-Fans   Low-Value Fans   Mid-Value Fans   High-Value Fans
(n = 5,982)   (n = 6,172)   (n = 11,139)   (n = 6,749)

2.1   **Average number of friends by Fan Value segment.** N = 30,042.
      Q: How many friends would you say you have?

fan segment. Moving from left to right, we see that Non-Fans average 21.1 friends, Low-Value Fans average 20.8, Mid-Value Fans average 27, and High-Value Fans average 35.6. This basic pattern held across all 11 surveys, no matter the season, no matter the context. And while we saw subtle variations in the average number of friends, the proportion between fan segments never changed.

Fig. 2.2

Not only do fans have more friends, but they also value those relationships more. The next chart shows the percentages of respondents that "greatly value" their friends from each origin point, meaning they rated five or six on a six-point scale. You'll see that at every origin point, the bigger a fan you are, the more likely you are to "greatly value" that friend group. The relative difference between segments is noticeable here, with the most dramatic lift appearing between Mid-Value and High-Value Fans.

Fig. 2.3

This holds for family members, as well. It turns out that bigger fans are more likely to "greatly value" their relationships with their mothers, fathers, siblings, and so on. Said another way: one way to improve the chances of having a solid relationship with your children is to pass down fandom. And one way to improve your relationship with your own parents is to invite them to a game. Sure, that's an oversimplification, but on balance, fandom seems to dramatically (and positively) impact family dynamics.

Fig. 2.4

If bigger fans have more friends and value those relationships more, it should come as no surprise that they also tend to interact with those friends more frequently. We defined these interactions broadly: from heart-to-heart conversations to short-and-sweet text messages. It should also be noted that these are general interactions, not necessarily about sports. We simply asked how often respondents engage with each group of friends. As the next chart indicates, the more engaged the fan, the more frequent the interaction.

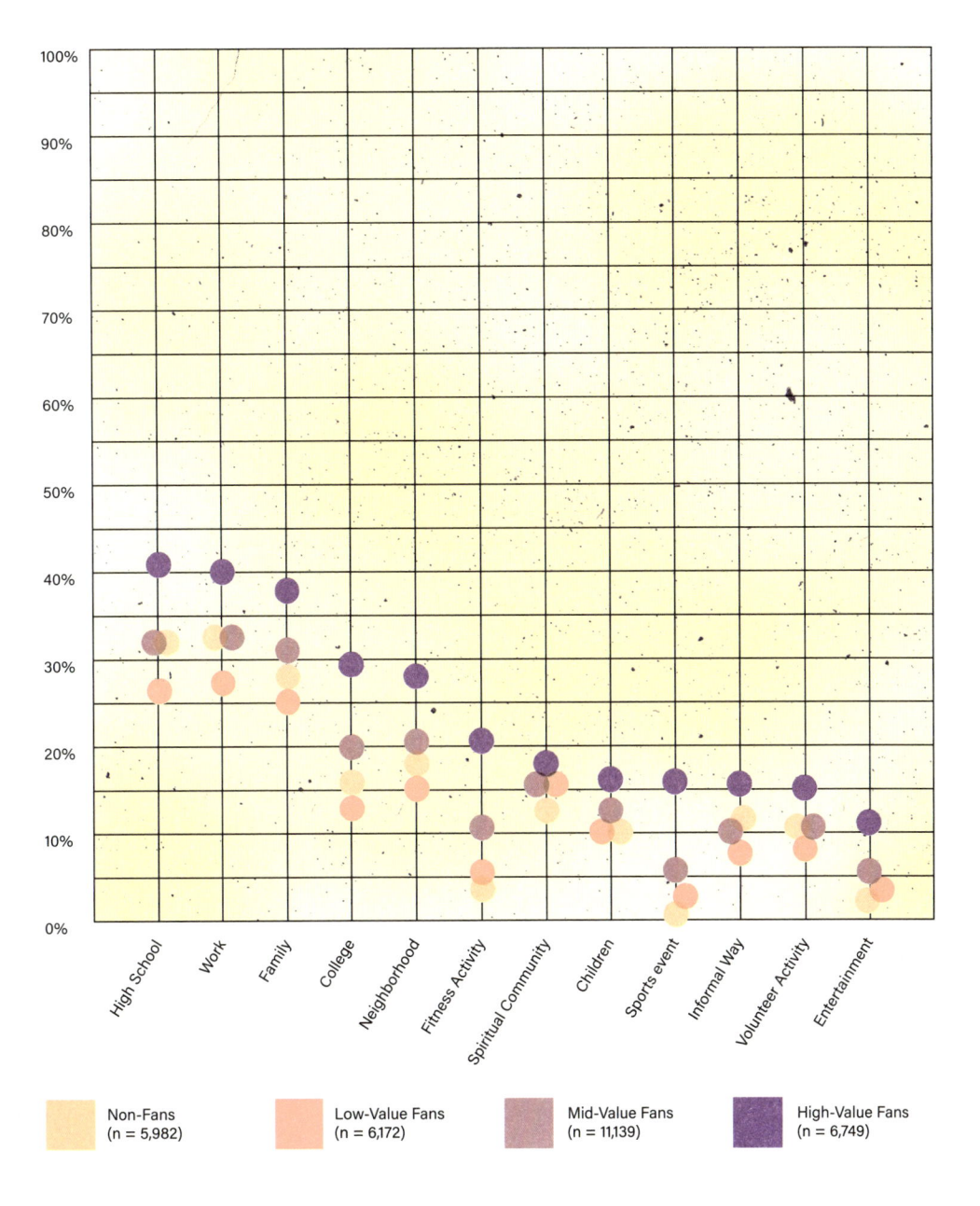

2.2   The percent who "greatly value" friendships from each origination point. N = 30,042.
Q: How much do you value the following friendships?

Legend:
- Non-Fans (n = 5,982)
- Low-Value Fans (n = 6,172)
- Mid-Value Fans (n = 11,139)
- High-Value Fans (n = 6,749)

Categories (x-axis): High School, Work, Family, College, Neighborhood, Fitness Activity, Spiritual Community, Children, Sports event, Informal Way, Volunteer Activity, Entertainment

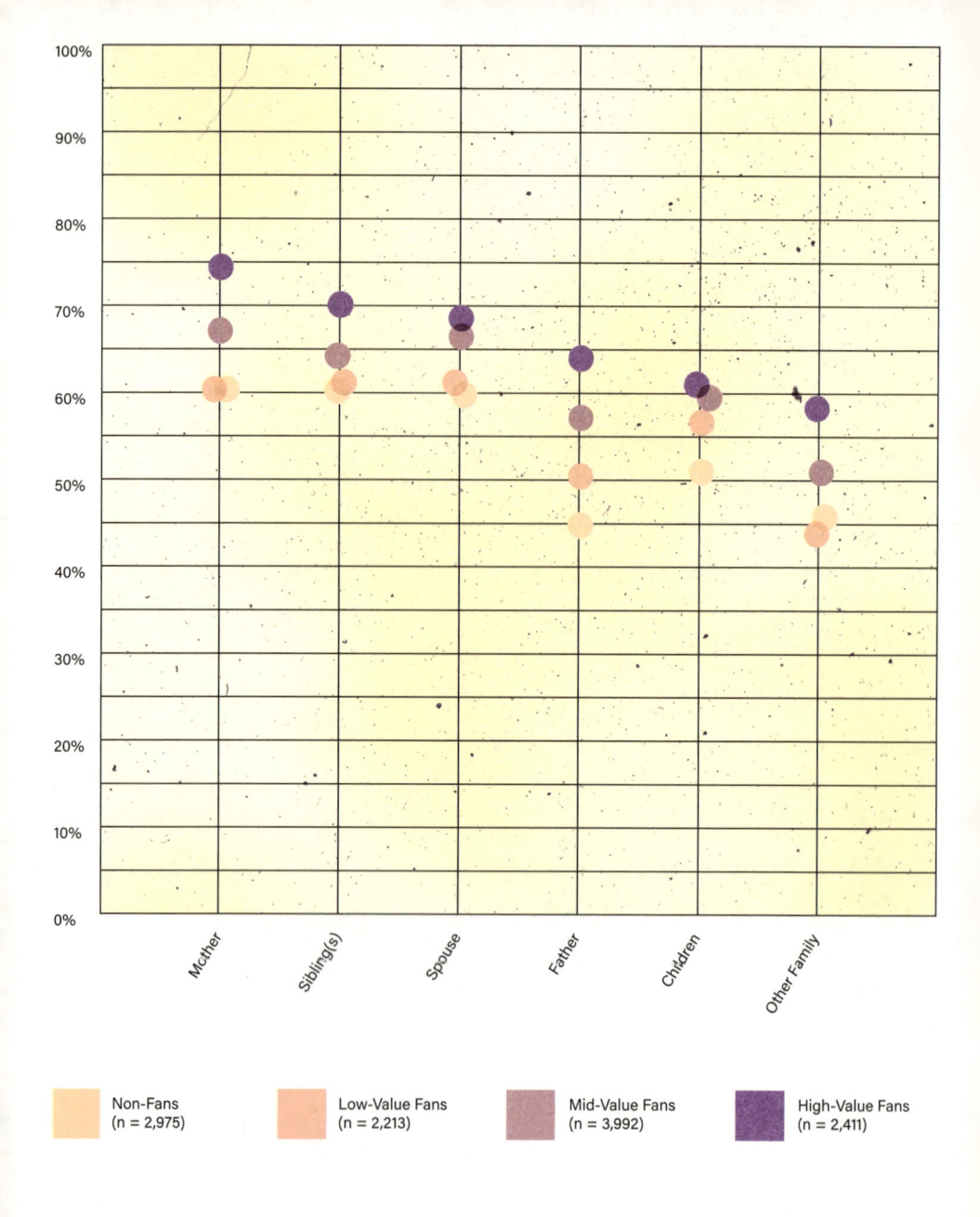

| | Non-Fans (n = 2,975) | Low-Value Fans (n = 2,213) | Mid-Value Fans (n = 3,992) | High-Value Fans (n = 2,411) |

2.3   **The percent who "greatly value" individual family members.** N = 11,591.
Q: Now, thinking of your family, how much do you value the following relationships?

FANS HAVE MORE FRIENDS

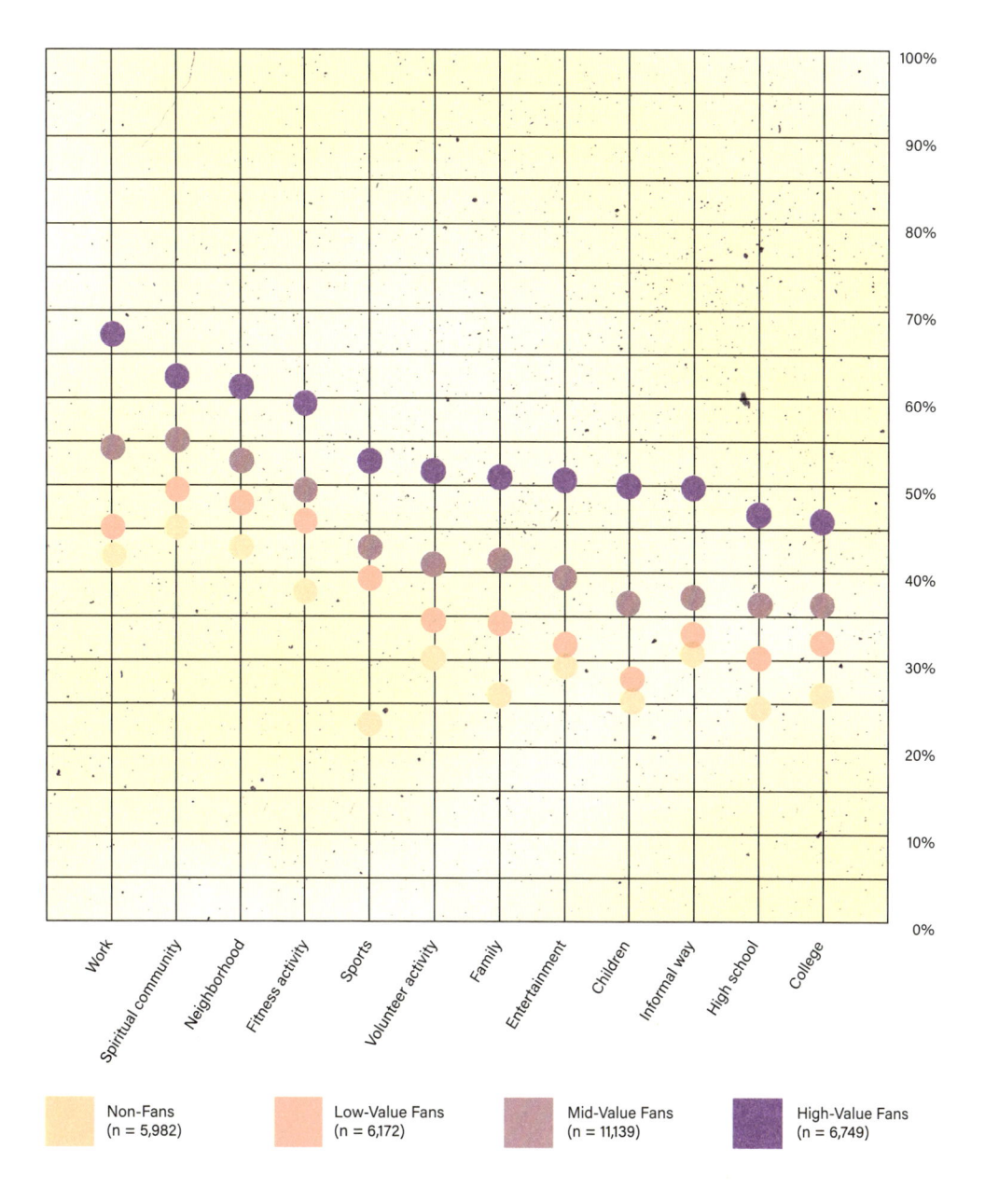

2.4 **The percent who interact at least weekly with friends from each origination point.** N = 30,042.
Q: How often would you say you interact with friends from the following sources?

It is important to note here that interactions do not operate in a linear fashion. Frequency is a force multiplier. That is, if you interact more frequently, then over time you will accumulate more and more individual interactions. So, for someone with a robust, active social network like Greg's, these interactions can add up quickly.

This explains, at least in part, why sports are such a powerful bonding agent: they give fans more opportunities to interact. As one fan put it in an interview at the beginning of the COVID-19 pandemic, "I guess I can always text a friend and ask how it's going, but that's kind of weird, especially just out of the blue on a Tuesday night. It's so much easier to say, 'Did you see that dunk?' because then we can just interact naturally. That's what I'm missing right now." This ability to seed and grow social interaction is the magic of sports, and the impact on estimated number of monthly interactions is significant. For example, Non-Fans average an estimated 204 monthly interactions, while High-Value Fans average 454 monthly interactions.

Hypothesis confirmed: fans have more friends, they value those relationships more, and they interact with those people more often.

But why? Is fandom the reason?

CAUSATION VS. CORRELATION

These same patterns manifested in survey after survey, with only slight variation. Every chart always looked the same. The natural question we had to ask ourselves, then, was: What other variables might influence this phenomenon? A variety of demographic variables are known to correlate to an increase in friendships. For instance, people who earn below $50K annually average 22.7 friends, while people who earn more than $100K average 31.2 friends. The same goes for college education (more education = more friends) and the presence of children under 18 in the home (more kids = more friends). All of these variables show some relationship, but what's the most influential variable?

Let's look at income first. In Figure 2.5, you'll see the number of friends broken out by fan segment and across income tiers. Notice that the same general pattern holds across the spectrum of fandom, from Non-Fans to High-Value Fans, regardless of income tier. Further, within that pattern, High-Value Fans always have more friends. In fact, High-Value Fans who earn less than $50K have more friends (31.9 average) than Mid-Value Fans who earn more than $100K (30.4 average).

Fig. 2.5

The same holds true for education. As you'll see, fandom positively impacts friendships at all education levels, and High-Value Fans with a high-school diploma have more friends than Mid-Value Fans with a college degree.

Fig. 2.6

We see the pattern again amongst people with children at home. Fandom positively impacts friendships regardless of the number of children, and High-Value Fans with no children have more friends than Mid-Value Fans with three or more children.

Fig. 2.7

So, no matter what demographic variable we evaluate, we see higher rates of friendship in higher-value fans, which suggests that fandom is the most influential variable.

Another question nagged us: Do fans have more friends because of sports, or do more-social people naturally gravitate to sports? In other words, what is the direction of causation? Ultimately, it's impossible to know. We didn't personality-test every respondent. More importantly, even if we had, would they have been able to tell us which came first: their robust social networks or their attraction to sports?

Here's what we do know: sports are a mainstream cultural force that penetrates a significant portion of our society, and fandom is not relegated to

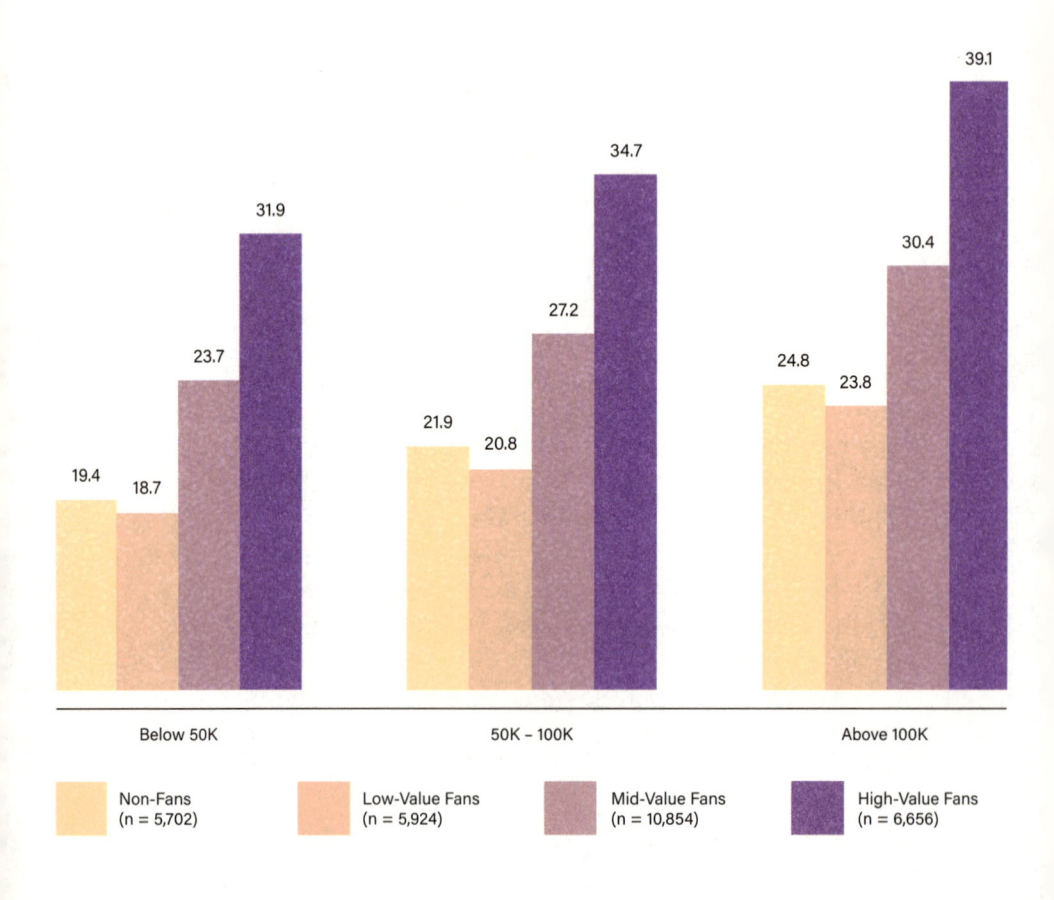

	Below 50K	50K – 100K	Above 100K
Non-Fans (n = 5,702)	19.4	21.9	24.8
Low-Value Fans (n = 5,924)	18.7	20.8	23.8
Mid-Value Fans (n = 10,854)	23.7	27.2	30.4
High-Value Fans (n = 6,656)	31.9	34.7	39.1

2.5 **Average number of friends by income.** N = 29,136.
Q1: How many friends would you say you have?
Q2: What is your annual household income?

any one personality type. Regardless of the results of your Meyers-Briggs test, one thing holds true: active engagement as a sports fan will grow your social network. This is not accidental or coincidental. This is the superpower of sports fandom, sparking connections between people and nurturing established relationships. Too often — and as we'll see in the chapters that follow, to our detriment — we overlook this fundamental truth.

For us, this paradigm shift was akin to a conversion. The scales fell from our eyes, and once we saw the true power of fandom, we could not unsee it.

Which brings us back to Greg Armstrong.

A RICH MAN

Greg Armstrong purchased his first season-ticket package for two reasons: he thought the Knicks were about to make a turnaround, and he wanted to share that experience with his children. We propose that it's the second part of that equation that drove him to continue purchasing season tickets for, as of this writing, thirty years.

Remember, Greg's fandom took root in the soil of one of his earliest and most significant relationships: the one with his older brother. The Knicks were their shared passion, a common cause, an anchor for their relationship. Throughout his youth, especially when he started going to Knicks games, sneaking down into the lower sections of The Garden, Greg was doing so with his friends. When he became a father, he almost unknowingly used the Knicks to nurture his relationship with his children. He thought he was, in his words, "passing down the fandom." But really, the Knicks were providing an opportunity for him to connect with his kids. When we spoke to him in 2021, Greg reflected, "My kids are growing up, they're going

                                                                                    45.0

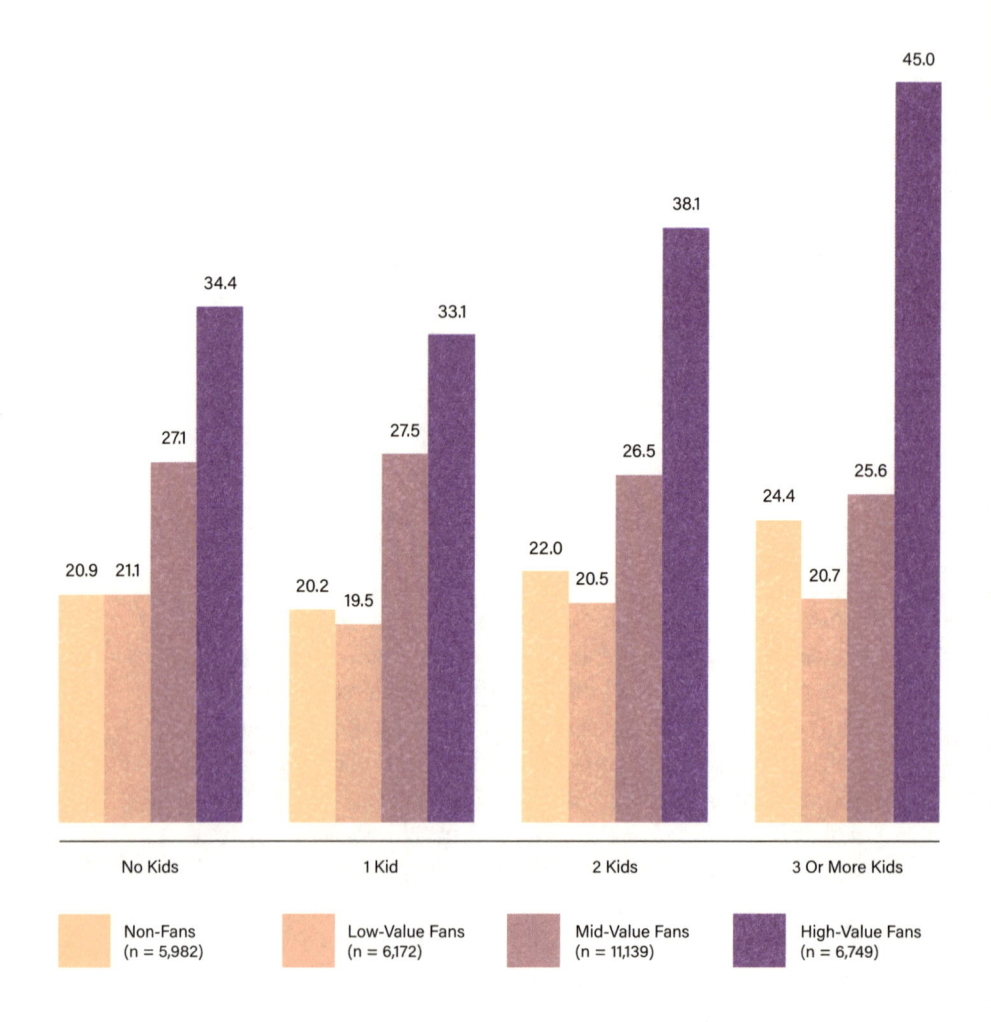

                                                                38.1

                                       33.1
                      34.4

              27.1   27.5   26.5   25.6
                                                                24.4
                                       22.0   20.5   20.7
      20.9 21.1   20.2   19.5

      No Kids   1 Kid   2 Kids   3 Or More Kids

  ■ Non-Fans   ■ Low-Value Fans   ■ Mid-Value Fans   ■ High-Value Fans
    (n = 5,982)   (n = 6,172)   (n = 11,139)   (n = 6,749)

2.7   **Average number of friends by presence of children ages < 18.** N = 30,042.
        Q1: How many friends would you say you have?
        Q2: How many children are you the parent of that are under 18 years old?

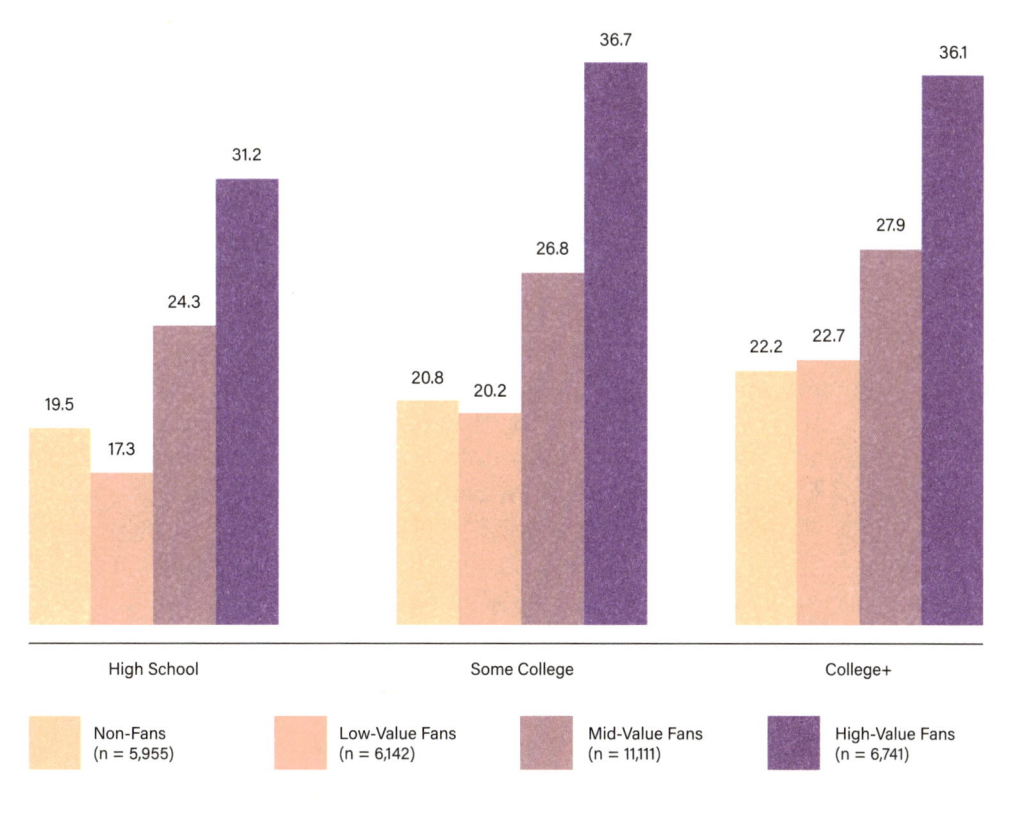

	High School	Some College	College+
Non-Fans	19.5	20.8	22.2
Low-Value Fans	17.3	20.2	22.7
Mid-Value Fans	24.3	26.8	27.9
High-Value Fans	31.2	36.7	36.1

Non-Fans (n = 5,955)
Low-Value Fans (n = 6,142)
Mid-Value Fans (n = 11,111)
High-Value Fans (n = 6,741)

2.6 **Average number of friends by education.** N = 29,949.
Q1: How many friends would you say you have?
Q2: What is the highest level of education you have completed?

to games, we're spending time together, and the bond between us — it's growing. Of course, we have times together at home, but going to games, even in a bad season, you have a good time at the game — you get to cheer and hug and high five."

When you look at Greg's purchase decision through the relationship lens, it makes perfect sense. The Knicks' record during any given year (or decade) becomes irrelevant, because this is about a father investing in his relationship with his children. The long commute from his home to The Garden becomes a feature, not a bug, because it means more time together. Each game becomes a collection of priceless moments shared between parent and child. Thirty-plus games a year will never be enough for Greg — because it's not about the game.

By Greg's estimate, he has attended more than five hundred games with at least one of his four sons. The youngest, a recent college graduate, is the biggest fan. "That's my sidekick," Greg says. "He's a passionate Knicks fan. He's carrying the torch. To be honest with you, it means everything in the world to me, the fact that my son, he wants to go. I'm not dragging him. It's way more than being with a friend, a buddy — he's my flesh and blood."

Fandom is too often trivialized as a bunch of amped-up, testosterone-driven meatheads investing too much energy into a silly game. From this point of view, minus the face paint and aggression, Greg's loyalty to the Knicks might look a lot like Puddy-the-face-painter's unhinged passion for the Devils.

Certainly, their vernacular is the same. When he was asked about his loyalty to the Knicks over the years in an interview on Fox 5, Greg explained, "There's days when you come to the games and they continue to lose, and each game you come in with a bright outlook, and you want them to win, so you just got to hang in there and just be a real fan and pray for the day when things turn around again." When talk turned to the 2021 playoff run, Greg gushed, "It's unbelievable right now, been waiting for this for eight long years. It's been frustrating, but it's going to be so exciting to get in my seat, with my son, and watch this game. The energy and the passion of being in MSG — it's going to be awesome."

When you look past the fan rhetoric, though, the stereotype dissolves, and Greg's real motivations become clear: he's looking forward to getting into his seat *with his son*. When asked what it was like to return to The Garden after the COVID-19 shutdown, he told Fox 5, "Going to games was a part of my life, so it was tough not being able to go. When we were actually able to get back in the building, it felt great. Even though it was only two thousand fans, it was still great. I know a lot of people that work here, my family, my friends — so it really felt great to get back." Again, we see his true focus: the people in the stands, not on the court.

At its core, Greg's fandom is a social accelerator that facilitates friendships and deepens family ties. When he walks into The Garden, he's walking into a web of meaningful relationships and continuing a legacy of social connection that began in his childhood. Moreover, fandom gives him something to talk about anywhere he goes, with nearly anyone he meets: his sons, his barber, his colleagues at work, and strangers on the subway. These daily interactions create a vibrant and fulfilling social life.

That was our theory, at least. When we reconnected with Greg in 2021, we played it back for him. Was it possible, we asked, that it wasn't passion for basketball or loyalty to the Knicks that motivated him to keep buying season tickets? Was it possible that he was actually investing in his social network, particularly his relationships with his sons? "I never thought of it that way," Greg responded. "But if you really analyze it, it makes sense that that's actually what's going on. I mean, I don't consciously do it, say, 'Let me put my money up, so I can make all these things happen,' but these are the effects."

We have received similar responses from every fan we have met along the way: first a flicker of recognition, then, unequivocally, "Yes, that's exactly what's going on." Whether we are conscious of it or not — and we ourselves were not at all conscious of it before we started this journey — by engaging in fan behaviors, we are generating a social currency that pays dividends not only in the arena but also far beyond it. This insight changed the way we think about the sports business, but far more importantly, it revolutionized the way we think about — and engage in — fandom. As the world around us became increasingly more disconnected and polarized, we embarked on a new mission: to bring people together, one fan at a time.

03 The Fandom Flywheel

In May 2018, the Supreme Court of the United States overturned the Professional and Amateur Sports Protection Act of 1992. The act had effectively outlawed sports betting nationwide, outside of a few states. The Court's ruling did not "legalize" sports betting, but it did defederalize prohibitions, granting individual states the authority to determine their own regulations. Between May 2018 and December 2021, 31 states legalized some form of sports betting, and as of this writing 16 others have legislation in process. This has opened the door for millions of fans to legally wager on games, greatly expanding the annual sports betting handle.

At the fan level, what sports betting looks like today depends upon the state. In some cases, wagering is as simple as downloading an app on your phone and making some picks. In others, placing a bet requires a trip to the local sportsbook. No matter what form betting takes, defederalization and rapid state-by-state legalization add another dimension to the fan experience. Ever curious about fans, we wanted to pop the hood on this activity to figure out what sports betting behavior is all about.

Initially, we entered into the space with some trepidation. Like so many people, we saw this most misunderstood of fan activities as the purview of shady bookies, insurmountable debt, and shattered kneecaps, replete with characters like Robert De Niro's Samuel "Ace" Rothstein, James Gandolfini's Tony Soprano, and Adam Sandler's Howard Ratner. The illicit cloud hanging over sports betting was clouding our thinking. We quickly saw that, similar to the way conventional thinking doesn't account for the social power of fandom, preconceived notions surrounding sports betting are also insufficient. Not only did our investigation dispel the stereotype, but our insight into sports bettors helped us understand how fandom operates.[6]

DEMYSTIFYING DEGENERATES

Though many bettors adopt a "degenerate" persona when they talk about betting, our interviews with hundreds of sports bettors revealed that the persona did not reflect reality. So, if today's sports bettors aren't dangerously indebted to the Mob and compulsively wagering their kids' college funds, then who are they?

Well, first off, they are sports fans. In fact, fandom is a necessary precondition for sports betting. What does that mean? Well, while not all fans are bettors, all bettors are fans. On average, the bigger the fan, the greater the interest in betting. That might seem obvious, but it is an important starting point as we seek to understand sports bettors.

To illustrate this fact, Figure 3.1 shows the relationship between fandom and betting interest. As the Fan Value Score increases from Non-Fan to High-Value Fan, so does betting interest. For example, 10% of respondents who had a Value Score of 5 are interested in betting. Moving up the scale, 35% of respondents who scored 20 are interested in betting, while 63% of respondents who scored 30 are interested. So, there is an obvious relationship between fandom level and interest in sports betting.

Fig. 3.1

But that's just *interest* in betting. How many of these fans are actually placing bets? The next graph illustrates how a given fan's likelihood of betting increases as their Value Score rises. Now, let's look at the distribution of bettors among Value segments. As Figure 3.3 illustrates, the vast majority of sports bettors (75%) are High-Value Fans, whereas only 1% of bettors are Low-Value Fans. Let's put those numbers into context. Only 27% of our sample are High-Value Fans, and yet they make up more than three-fourths of all bettors. Low-Value Fans, on the other hand, account for 18% of our sample, and only account for 1% of all bettors. Again, while not all fans are bettors, all bettors are fans.

Fig. 3.2

Fig. 3.3

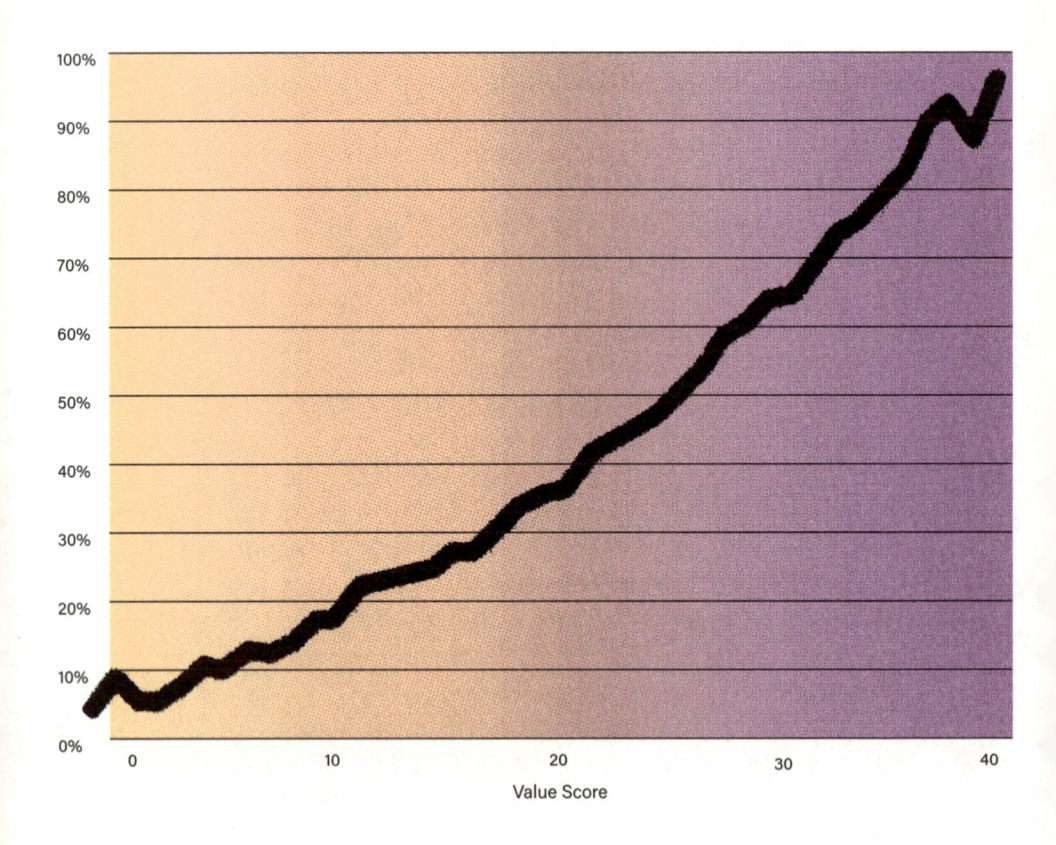

3.1 **The percent who are interested in betting at each Value Score interval.** N = 35,449.
Q: How interested would you say you are in betting on sports?
* Value Score calculated without the two-point bonus provided for indicating betting on sports. Therefore, the Value Score range is 0–51 instead of 0–53. 40 and above on Value Score have been combined due to lower incidence on the extreme ends of Value Score.

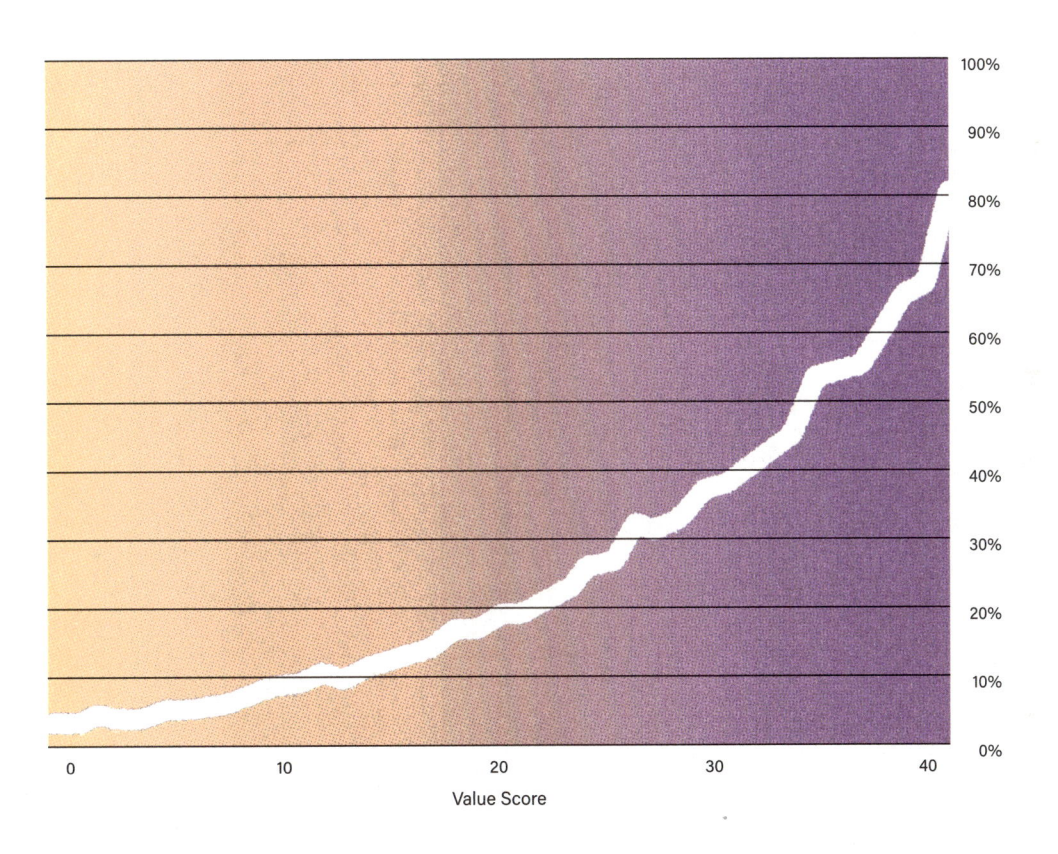

3.2 **The percent who bet on sports at each Value Score interval.** N = 35,449.
Q: Thinking of the last year, which of the following activities have you done in conjunction with the sports you follow? *Placed a bet at a sportsbook/casino/bookie.*
* Value Score calculated without the two-point bonus provided for indicating betting on sports. Therefore, the Value Score range is 0–51 instead of 0–53. 40 and above on Value Score have been combined due to lower incidence on the extreme ends of Value Score.

Distribution of Fans in Non-Bettors
(n = 20,604)

- High-Value Fans 27%
- Mid-Value Fans 55%
- Low-Value Fans 18%

Distribution of Fans Among Bettors
(n = 5,143)

- High-Value Fans 75%
- Mid-Value Fans 24%
- Low-Value Fans 1%

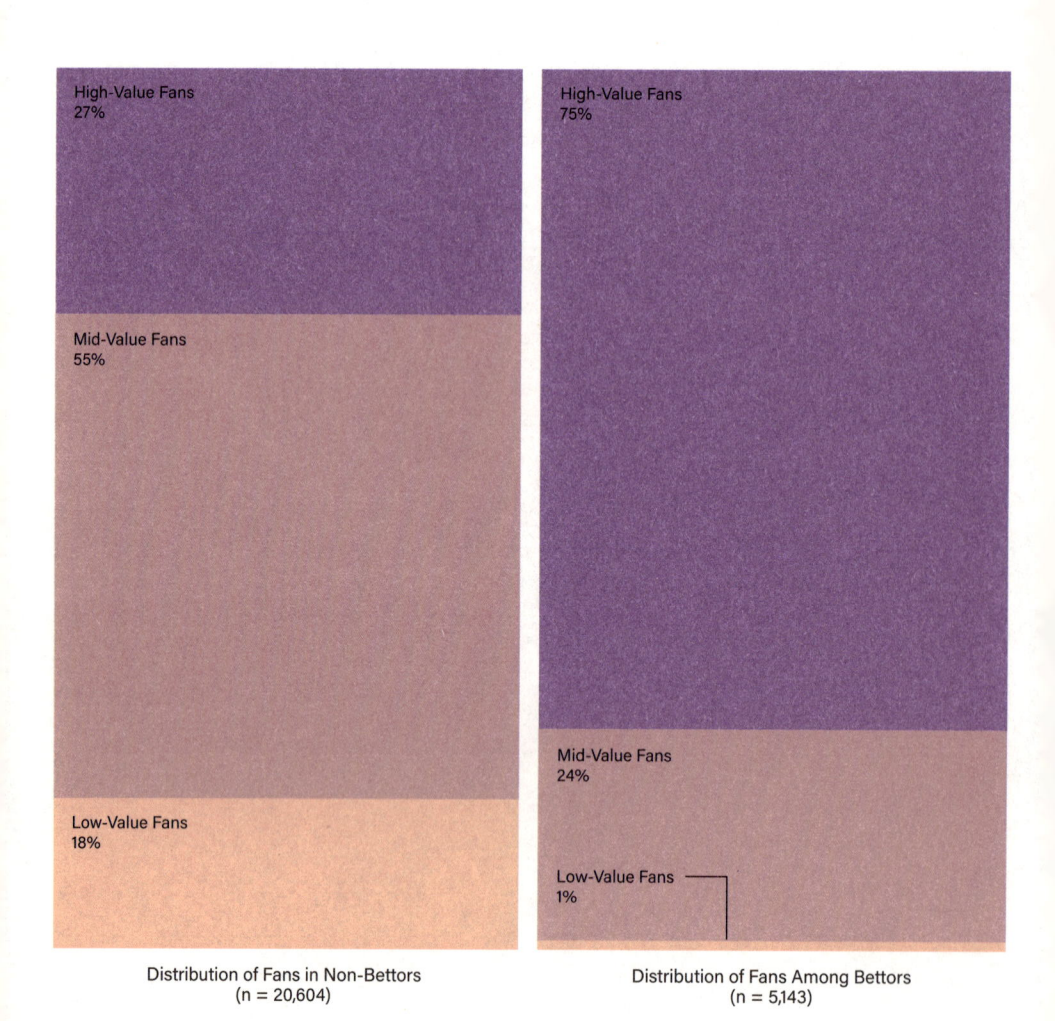

3.3 **Distribution of Fan Value segments among Non-Bettors and Bettors.** N = 25,747.
Q: Thinking of the last year, which of the following activities have you done in conjunction with the sports you follow? *Placed a bet at a sportsbook/casino/bookie.*

THE FANDOM FLYWHEEL

These distinctions are important because they help us make more accurate comparisons between non-bettors and bettors. Let's start with the demographics. Comparing non-bettors and bettors, we see quite the opposite of the "degenerate" stereotype. In fact, bettors are more likely than non-bettors to be married, to have children, to be college educated, to be employed full-time, and to earn more than $100K per year. Bettors are even slightly more likely than non-bettors to attend religious service frequently.

Fig. 3.4

As we saw in Chapter 2, these demographic markers have a positive relationship with fandom in general. Because we know bettors skew High-Value, one could assume that these demographic characteristics are a function of fandom generally and not betting specifically. In the next chart, we look at the same demographic attributes, split between non-bettors and bettors, but only among High-Value Fans. As you will see, even among High-Value Fans, bettors remain more likely than non-bettors to be married, to have children, to be college educated, to be employed full-time, and to earn $100K+ per year.

Fig. 3.5

No matter how we slice it, sports bettors have a demographic profile that runs counter to the common stereotype. These are not "degenerates" risking the mortgage against the odds. They are not down-on-their-luck losers taking desperate chances to catapult themselves out of debt. They're not rabbit's foot–rubbing hopefuls with dollar signs in their eyes. In fact, it's quite the opposite. But these demographics are only part of the story.

BETTORS SOCIALIZE MORE

In Chapter 2, we looked to Greg, the Knicks season-ticket holder, to illustrate how social connections fuel what — on the surface — seems like an expensive, time-consuming, and altogether irrational season-ticket purchase. We found that the basic underlying

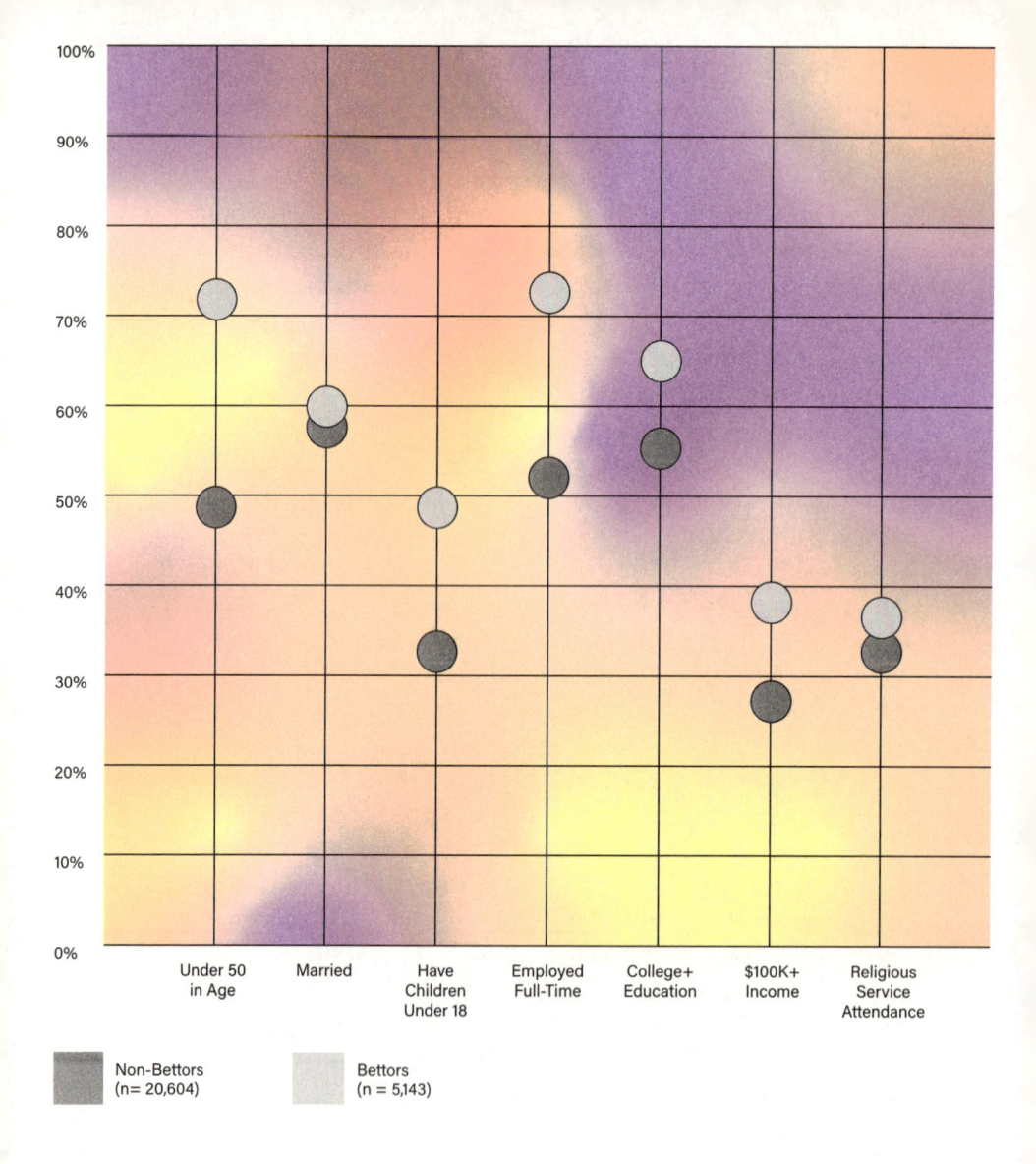

	Under 50 in Age	Married	Have Children Under 18	Employed Full-Time	College+ Education	$100K+ Income	Religious Service Attendance
Bettors (n = 5,143)	72%	60%	49%	73%	65%	38%	37%
Non-Bettors (n = 20,604)	49%	58%	33%	52%	55%	27%	33%

3.4 **The percent of Non-Bettors and Bettors who meet specific demographic criteria.** N = 25,747. Q: Thinking of the last year, which of the following activities have you done in conjunction with the sports you follow? *Placed a bet at a sportsbook/casino/bookie.*

THE FANDOM FLYWHEEL

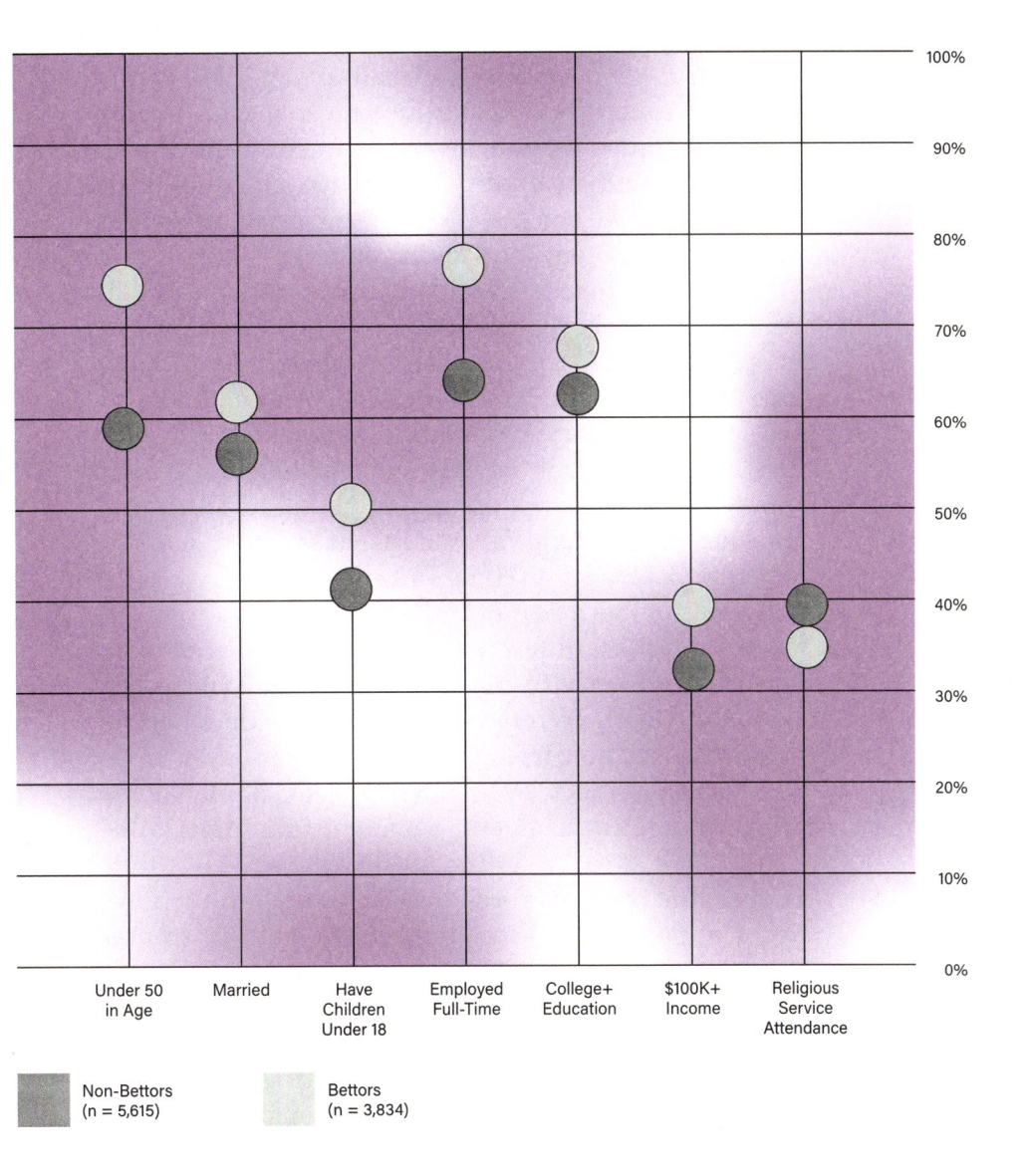

	100%
	90%
	80%
	70%
	60%
	50%
	40%
	30%
	20%
	10%
	0%

Under 50 in Age | Married | Have Children Under 18 | Employed Full-Time | College+ Education | $100K+ Income | Religious Service Attendance

Non-Bettors (n = 5,615)
Bettors (n = 3,834)

3.5 **The percent of Non-Bettors and Bettors who meet specific demographic criteria among High-Value Fans.** N = 9,449.
Q: Thinking of the last year, which of the following activities have you done in conjunction with the sports you follow? *Placed a bet at a sportsbook/casino/bookie.*

motivation driving Greg's decades-long decision to buy season tickets was *belonging*. Greg isn't buying tickets so much as he's investing in connection with other fans and in quality time with his sons. This changed how we see the Gregs of the world, as well as how we think about fandom in general.

Fig. 3.6

What happens when we apply this same social lens to sports betting? As higher-value sports fans, it stands to reason that bettors should be tapping into the social benefits of fandom. As you'll see in the following chart, non-bettors average 27.9 friends and bettors average 32.3 friends. We should expect this because most bettors are High-Value Fans, and we know that High-Value Fans have more friends. When we look only at High-Value Fans, the friend gap between non-bettors and bettors closes.

Fig. 3.7

The real difference between non-bettor and bettor social activity appears when you look at the frequency of their interactions. We see that bettors interact with their friends almost twice as often as do non-bettors. In fact, even when we looked only at the High-Value Fans segment, we found that High-Value non-bettors average 409 monthly interactions, while High-Value bettors average 521 monthly interactions. So, it appears that something about betting creates more social interaction. What's going on?

THE FANDOM FLYWHEEL

We now understand that sports betting is far from the seedy, outlier activity we once thought it was. In fact, it is the activity that best illustrates a phenomenon we have come to call the *fandom flywheel*. But before we go any further, we need to explain the flywheel concept.

If you've ever been to a playground with a merry-go-round, you've encountered a flywheel in its simplest form. Imagine you load about three hundred pounds' worth of rambunctious children onto

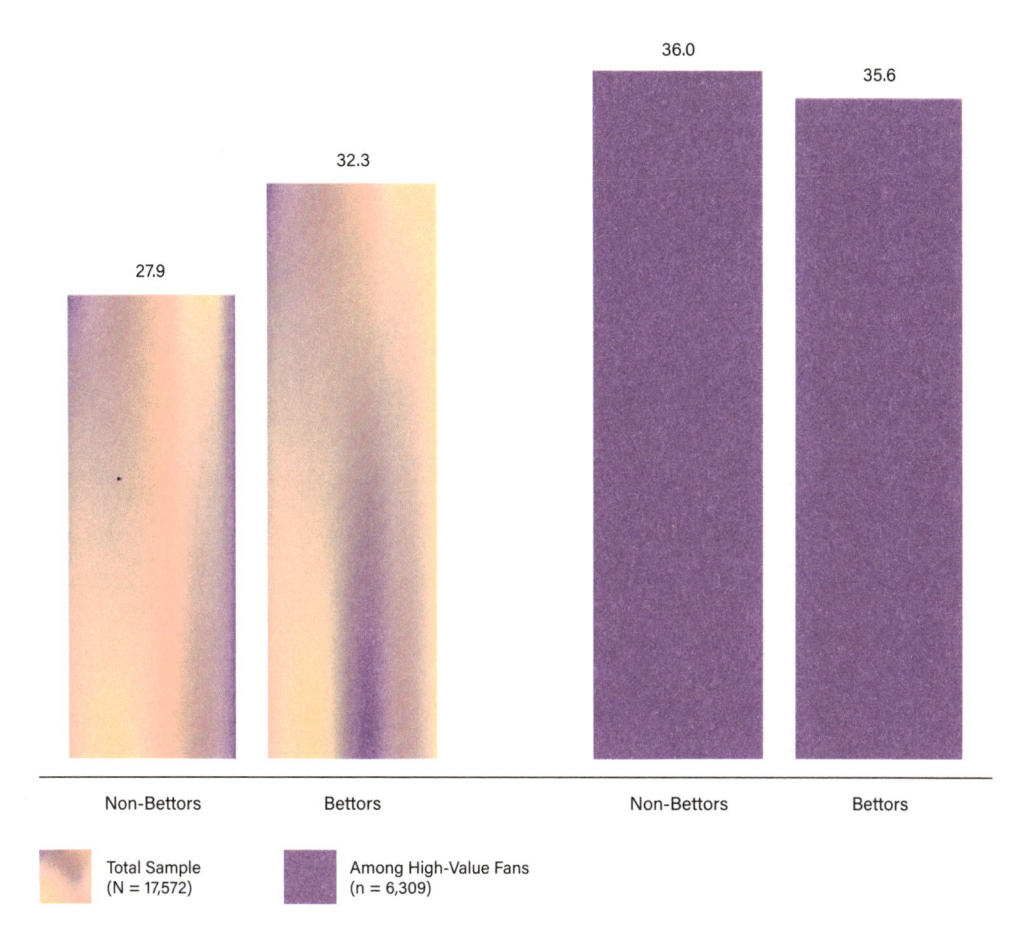

	Non-Bettors	Bettors	Non-Bettors	Bettors
Total Sample (N = 17,572)	27.9	32.3		
Among High-Value Fans (n = 6,309)			36.0	35.6

3.6 **Average number of friends for Non-Bettors and Bettors among total sample and High-Value Fans.**
N = 17,572.
Q1: How many friends would you say you have from each of these origination points?
Q2: Thinking of the last year, which of the following activities have you done in conjunction with the sports you follow? *Placed a bet at a sportsbook/casino/bookie.*

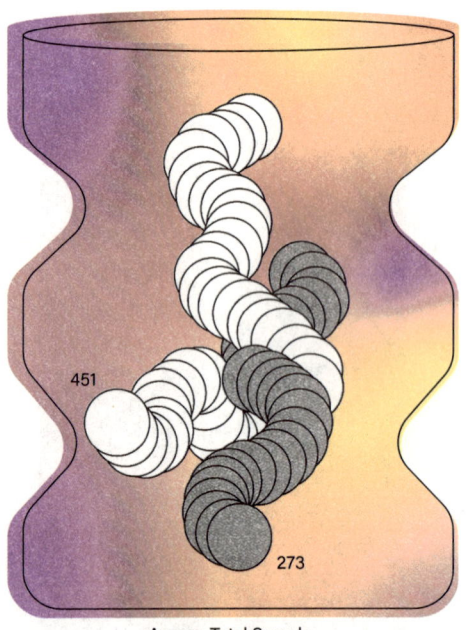

Among Total Sample
(N = 21,213)

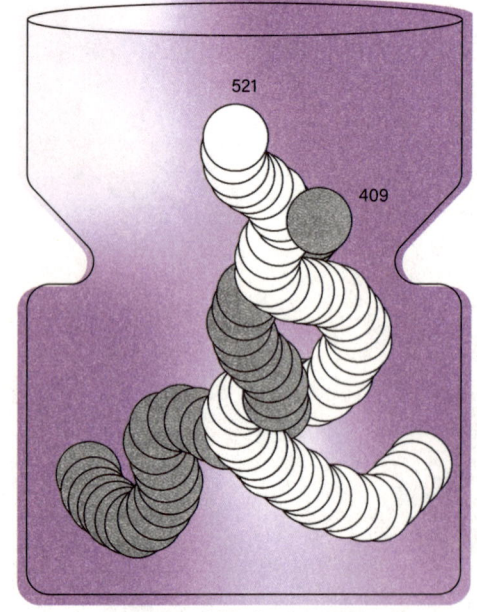

521
409

Among High-Value Fans Only
(n = 6,171)

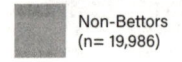

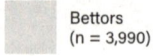

451
273

■ Non-Bettors (n= 19,986)   ■ Bettors (n = 3,990)

3.7 **Estimated number of monthly interactions for Non-Bettors and Bettors among Total Sample and High-Value Fans.** N = 21,213.
Q1: How often would you say you interact with friends from the following sources?
Q2: Thinking of the last year, which of the following activities have you done in conjunction with the sports you follow? *Placed a bet at a sportsbook/casino/bookie.*

a circular metal platform about eight feet in diameter. They grip tight to handrails meant to keep them from flinging off. If you're the workhorse tasked with getting this thing going, you dig your feet into the dirt, grab onto a handrail, lean your full weight into it, and slowly, one step after another, start rotating the platform to the squealing soundtrack of "Faster! Faster! Faster!" The first few rotations are a slog. But as you keep pushing, the disk starts to turn faster. Eventually, momentum kicks in, the load seems lighter, your feet move faster, and you begin running alongside the spinning disk until you can no longer keep up. And then, you let go and the children are a blur speeding past you, the merry-go-round propelling itself forward.

In his seminal book, *Good to Great*, Jim Collins applies this flywheel concept to the effort it takes to achieve long-term, sustained business success.[7] He writes, "Imagine that your task is to get the flywheel rotating on the axle for as fast and as long as possible." The trick, as Collins points out, is this: No one "big push" gets the flywheel spinning. Rather, it's the cumulative effect of many "small pushes" that eventually add up to big results. Collins is describing the impact that compounding returns have on consistent, sustained effort.

In Brad Stone's *The Everything Store*, an account of Amazon's rise, the author describes a meeting between Collins, Jeff Bezos, and the Amazon management team during the company's early days.[8] He writes:

> Drawing on Collins' concept of a flywheel, or self-reinforcing loop, Bezos and his lieutenants sketched their own virtuous cycle, which they believed powered their business. It went something like this: lower prices led to more customer visits. More customers increased the

volume of sales and attracted more commission-paying, third-party sellers to the site. That allowed Amazon to get more out of fixed costs, like the fulfillment centers and the servers needed to run the website. This greater efficiency then enabled it to lower prices further. Feed any part of this flywheel, they reasoned, and it should accelerate the loop.

The "loop" is the key component here. Essentially, X causes Y, which in turn influences X, and so on. A flywheel leverages a positive feedback loop: The faster the flywheel spins, the more energy it generates; the more energy it generates, the faster it spins. A flywheel can also fall victim to a negative feedback loop: The slower the flywheel spins, the less energy it generates; the less energy it generates, the slower it spins. "Small pushes" + "positive feedback loop" = sustained momentum. It is precisely this type of momentum that has famously propelled companies like Amazon — and Apple and Disney, to name just three[9] — to tremendous success.

So, what does all this have to do with fans? Think of your own fandom for a moment. What was the "first push" that set it in motion? What "positive feedback" did you receive from those early experiences? What "small push actions" did you take in response to that feedback? And perhaps most importantly, who was involved in those early fan experiences? No matter where it started, your fandom has been propelled forward by a feedback loop between fan activities and social engagement.

Sports can enhance a fan's social life in three distinct ways:

First, sports act as a bonding agent that galvanizes relationships. For example, sports can be the foundation of your relationship with a parent, sibling, or neighbor: It's the thing you talk about, the activity you engage in together, the backdrop for some of your fondest memories.

Second, sports anchor social interactions that otherwise would not take place, like when your college basketball team's Cinderella run gives you a valid excuse to text an old roommate you haven't talked to for years, or the retirement of a franchise player has you on the phone with your father, reminiscing about career highlights.

Third, sports imbue individuals with a tremendous amount of social capital. Just think about how informed takes on the playoffs — any playoffs — give you something to talk about at a backyard barbecue, or how even minimal MLB knowledge can open the door to a conversation with a barista wearing a Cardinals cap.

This relationship between fandom and social interaction creates a feedback loop. As a fan engages in more fan activities, they have more social interactions, which inspires more fan engagement. Momentum builds. As they deepen their sports engagement, they grow their knowledge base and their cache of fan stories, which opens the door to more sports-related social interactions. The fan flywheel is now spinning freely, with this positive feedback loop incentivizing fans to lean into their fandom, generating more social interactions, which in turn incentivizes engagement in more fan activities. And on and on the flywheel spins.

Perhaps more clearly than any other fan activity, sports betting shows the fan flywheel in action. The incentive — whether bettors are conscious of it or not — is social. Just think about what a single bet can spur. Imagine a fan who draws from years of knowledge to place a bet on a single game. She gets together with a friend to watch, and the bet now gives her other angles to talk about the game (weather, injuries, hot streaks, etc.). Say the two friends decide to watch the game together at a bar, and the other patrons get wind of the bet. All the research the bettor did to place the bet spills out in conversations with other patrons at the bar. She can talk about the bet itself, or she can simply infuse her betting rationale into takes about the game: "This quarterback always struggles in cold weather." Now, everyone around her is talking about the game, debating the line, analyzing positional matchups. Someone says she bets. Another offers his own prognostication. The bartender chimes in with a bad beat story from the previous weekend. The shared interest in the room blooms. Everyone is engaged, everyone is connecting. And all this social momentum blossomed from a single "small push" activity.

Now consider that, for most sports bettors, betting is rarely a single transaction, but rather a whole host of "small push" activities — researching bets, listening to betting-focused podcasts, placing multiple bets, watching the games they bet on, joining pick 'em pools. All of these activities pay off with more social interaction, which generates more engagement in fandom that, in turn, creates more social interaction. And so the flywheel spins.

That's the flywheel in motion: Place a bet, interact with others, go on the ride, celebrate or commiserate, rinse, repeat. If betting is contained within reasonable financial boundaries, the sum of this activity has a net positive impact on bettors. Namely, it creates more frequent and more vibrant social interactions.

Our intention here is not to advocate for sports betting, per se, but to shed light on the way fandom works: Fan activities pull you deeper into fandom, which creates more social interactions, which incentivizes more fan activity, and so on. Sports betting brought the fandom flywheel to life for us, but the flywheel works in the same way with other fan activities, too. Let's broaden the scope and consider those.

Do activity ● **Do not do activity**

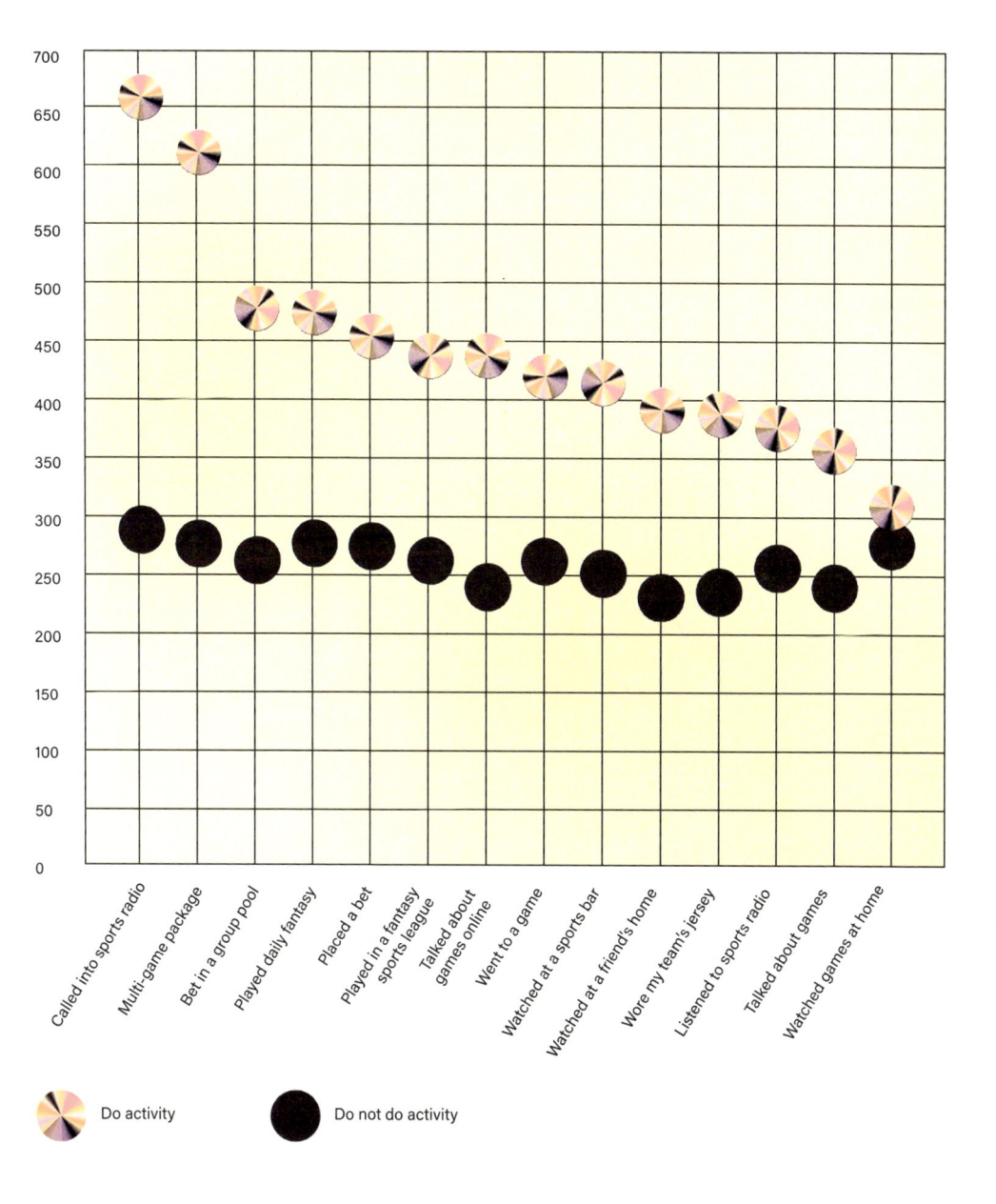

3.8 **Average number of estimated monthly interactions based on activity participation.** N = 21,213.
Q: How often would you say you interact with friends from the following sources?
Q2: Thinking of the last year, which of the following activities have you done in conjunction with the sports you follow? *Placed a bet at a sportsbook/casino/bookie.*

Fig. 3.8

If we look again at the measure of "total monthly interactions," what's clear is that you don't have to be a sports bettor to experience the social benefits of fandom. You simply have to engage in more activities. Among all fans, each of the activities listed in Figure 3.8 leads to more social interactions. For example, fans who do not participate in a fantasy league average 264 total monthly interactions, while fans who do average 439. It's the presence of the activity — the increased engagement — that, in turn, generates more social interactions.

THE ACCIDENTAL BOOKIE

Raised in a small town in Italy in the 1980s, Marco grew up playing soccer. But when high school graduation came, his soccer days ended. In Italy, you either play ball, or you go to school. You don't do both. College sports, athletic scholarships — they weren't an option. Marco's mother had impressed upon him that education was important, and sports were for fun, so he headed off to college, pursing a dual degree that allowed him to study for the first two years in Italy and the second two years abroad.

For those second two years, Marco landed in Boston, across the street from Fenway Park. That was in 2005. "I had no idea Fenway was such a big deal." Though he had some familiarity with baseball, he had heard only of the Yankees. During his two years in Boston, he confessed, "I never went to see the Red Sox." He had too much on his mind to bother with sports. He shrugged: "I had to figure out English first."

At the end of his stint in Boston, Marco accepted a six-month internship, and then a full-time position, at Merrill Lynch in New York. This is where his true education in American sports began. "My initial bosses at Merrill were both baseball fans. One was a Mets fan, and the other was a Phillies fan, and so I naturally became a Yankees fan to antagonize them."

The Yankees were doing well at the time, and Marco attended a few games with his colleagues. But for a guy whose sports rhythm was set to the constant motion of soccer, baseball seemed more like "an interesting social experiment" than an exciting sport to watch.

Then Marco switched work groups and found himself among a bunch of (American) football fans. To join in their discussions, he started watching some football. "Coming from Italy, I didn't have a lot in common with a lot of Americans, but I found a lot of appreciation for football players in terms of their physicality, the speed, the techniques. Despite the game stopping a lot, it was a lot more interesting to me than baseball ever was." As it happened, that year the Patriots were on fire, ending their regular season 16–0. "I got interested in a team that could make history," Marco said, "so I hosted a Super Bowl party."

Spoiler alert: the Patriots lost. But Marco, in search of social connection with his colleagues, had pushed the fandom flywheel. And it started to spin.

The next season, he added another fan activity: joining a fantasy football league. "It was a big opportunity for me to get closer to other people, to have something in common to talk about. It would force me also to pay more attention and understand the game better because the rules are complicated."

As the flywheel gained momentum, Marco's social connections grew, and his fandom deepened. Watching NFL RedZone and managing a fantasy football team, in combination, became a great way for him to become more knowledgeable about the NFL in general. "It definitely gets you to follow more and appreciate the sport more. Initially I was doing season-long fantasy football, where you have a draft at the beginning of the year. That involves a lot of up-front work and then maintenance over the weeks, but that caused too much frustration related to luck and injuries, so I moved to daily fantasy, where you get an opportunity to build your team every week. That requires you to become a much better observer of trends, and that got me more excited about certain players."

In 2018, when Marco and a few colleagues founded their own business, he immediately recognized an opportunity to bring the group together: He started a fantasy football league with them. He remained active in the Merrill Lynch league and in the new one, because together they allowed him "to network and stay in touch with a lot of different people."

Meanwhile, Marco discovered that he and a work friend shared a passion that predated his immigration to America: golf. The two began discussing golfers, playing together, and inviting others into their conversations. As that added activity accelerated the flywheel, friendships grew. Marco and his buddies began meeting up to watch tournaments together on TV.

Then, on June 11, 2018, a new fan activity appeared: Sports betting became legal in New Jersey. Marco wasn't a bettor, but he was a resident of New Jersey, so some of his friends at work, who lived in non-betting New York, began asking him to place bets on their behalf. "Until very recently, I was the one only who could put in bets, so I was basically the bookie."

Why did a non-bettor get involved in this process? Because he loved the interactions that betting sparked among his colleagues: the debates, the hot takes, the discussions, the live-texting during games, celebrating wins, commiserating losses, talking trash. His involvement in fantasy leagues had improved his understanding of the sport, which prepared him for in-depth conversations about each week's games, thus making him an essential member of the betting group beyond his "bookie" role. All of these different fan activities — Sundays watching RedZone, the fantasy leagues, the sports betting — resulted in more social interaction, which only incentivized deeper fan engagement. Marco's fan flywheel might have started slowly, but once it gained momentum, it started to spin freely, and his social connections flourished.

More importantly for Marco, betting gave him something positive to talk about with his colleagues. "There are things that don't make us happy about work, and this is a way to stay in touch after work, and not just complain about work. For me it's a good way to have something else to share."

Once again, this enhanced engagement in fan activities paid social dividends. Marco's friendships within the betting group grew beyond watching a game at a bar, debating who would win or lose over a business lunch, or goading via text during games. "One of the guys I talk with about betting, he has four tickets to the Masters. His father could not go with him [so]... he gave it to me." Attending the golf tournament has been a dream for Marco, and now it's coming true, with a good friend, thanks to the momentum of the fan flywheel.

In the end, Marco sees the benefits of the flywheel in his personal and work lives. "Becoming close friends outside of work makes it easier to collaborate and work well together. When you become friends, then you become more accountable to each other. You don't want to let each other down." In his experience, "People who bet together, stay together."

FANDOM'S INTRINSIC BENEFITS

This flywheel we're talking about — it's not trivial. It doesn't merely pull you into buying jerseys, or watching more games, or deepening your sports knowledge (although it does do those things). It pulls you into initiating more social interactions. And that, we suspect, is where the real payoff lies.

George Vallaint, principal investigator in The Grant Study, would agree. The Grant Study of

16%	20%	25%	34%

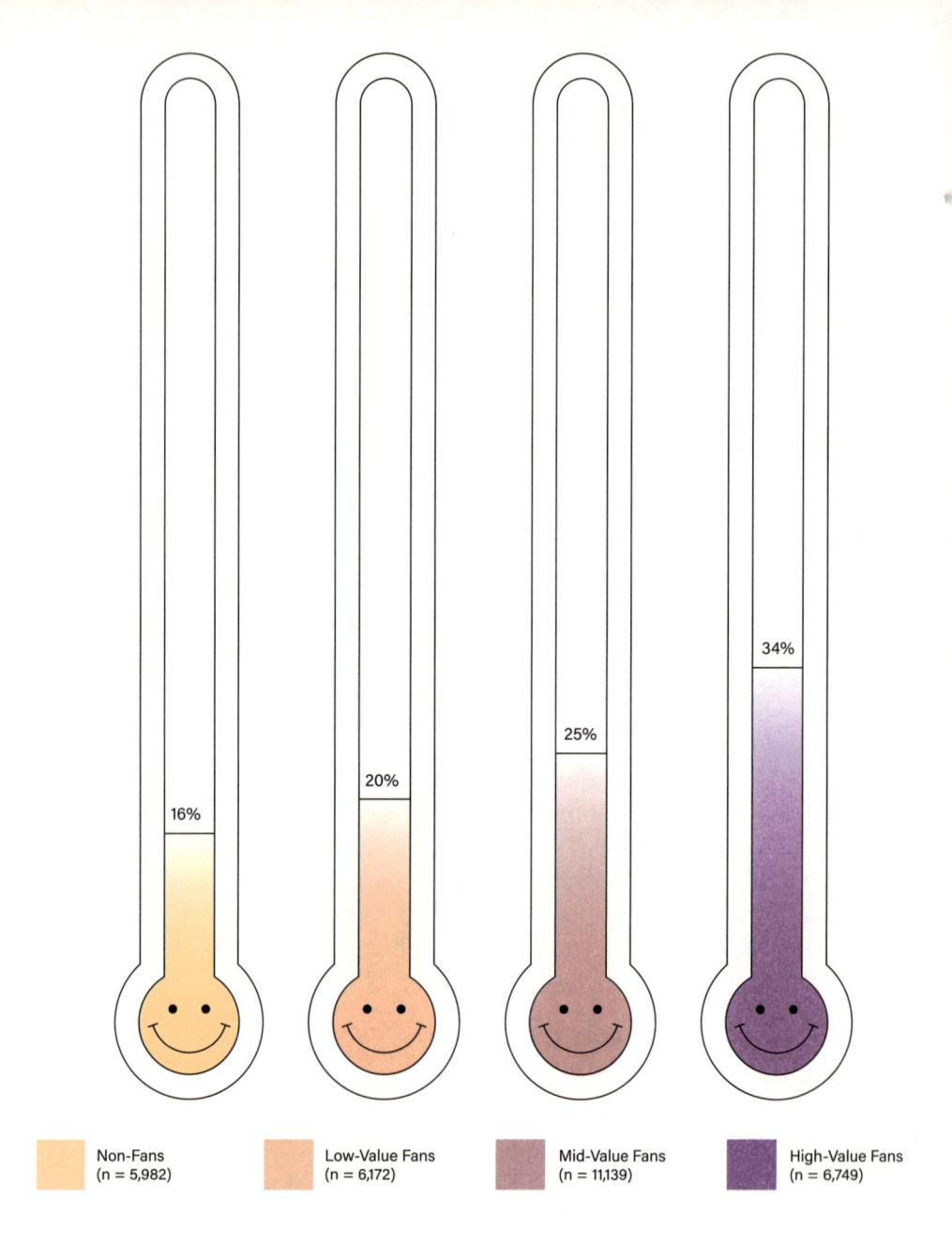

■ Non-Fans (n = 5,982)   ■ Low-Value Fans (n = 6,172)   ■ Mid-Value Fans (n = 11,139)   ■ High-Value Fans (n = 6,749)

3.9 **The percent who are very happy.** N = 30,042.
Q: Generally, how would you say things are these days in your life? Would you say that you are very happy, pretty happy, or not too happy?

THE FANDOM FLYWHEEL

Adult Development, which began in 1938, followed the lives of 268 men, all Harvard graduates, for 75 years, analyzing various components of their health and wellbeing.[10] When asked in 2008, "What have you learned from the Grant Study men?" Vallaint responded, "That the only thing that really matters in life are your relationships to other people."[11]

Knowing that fandom increases social interactions, we leaned into the idea that it could also elevate fans' sense of wellness. We began studying wellness-related social science and incorporating wellbeing measures into our own research. Soon, the cascading benefits of fans' rich social lives became clear. In what follows we highlight the impact of fandom across five wellness markers: happiness, satisfaction, optimism, gratitude, and confidence.

To measure happiness, we borrowed a scale from the Pew Research Center, an organization that regularly tracks happiness using a simple three-point scale: Very Happy, Pretty Happy, Not Too Happy. In the chart to the left, you will see a familiar pattern: the bigger the fan, the higher the level of happiness. Just over a third (34%) of High-Value Fans described themselves as very happy, compared to 25% of Mid-Value Fans and 20% of Low-Value Fans. More precisely, the bigger the fan, the more social interaction; the more social interaction, the happier the person. It's the additional socializing that fandom inherently spurs that leads to this increased happiness.

Fig. 3.9

Next, we employed a life satisfaction scale, also from Pew, asking respondents to rate their satisfaction with life in three areas: their family, their community, and their personal financial situation. With this added level of detail, we see even more dramatic differences in wellbeing between Non-Fans and High-Value Fans.

Fig. 3.10

We turned to Pew yet again to measure optimism, asking respondents to imagine how various

Fig. 3.10

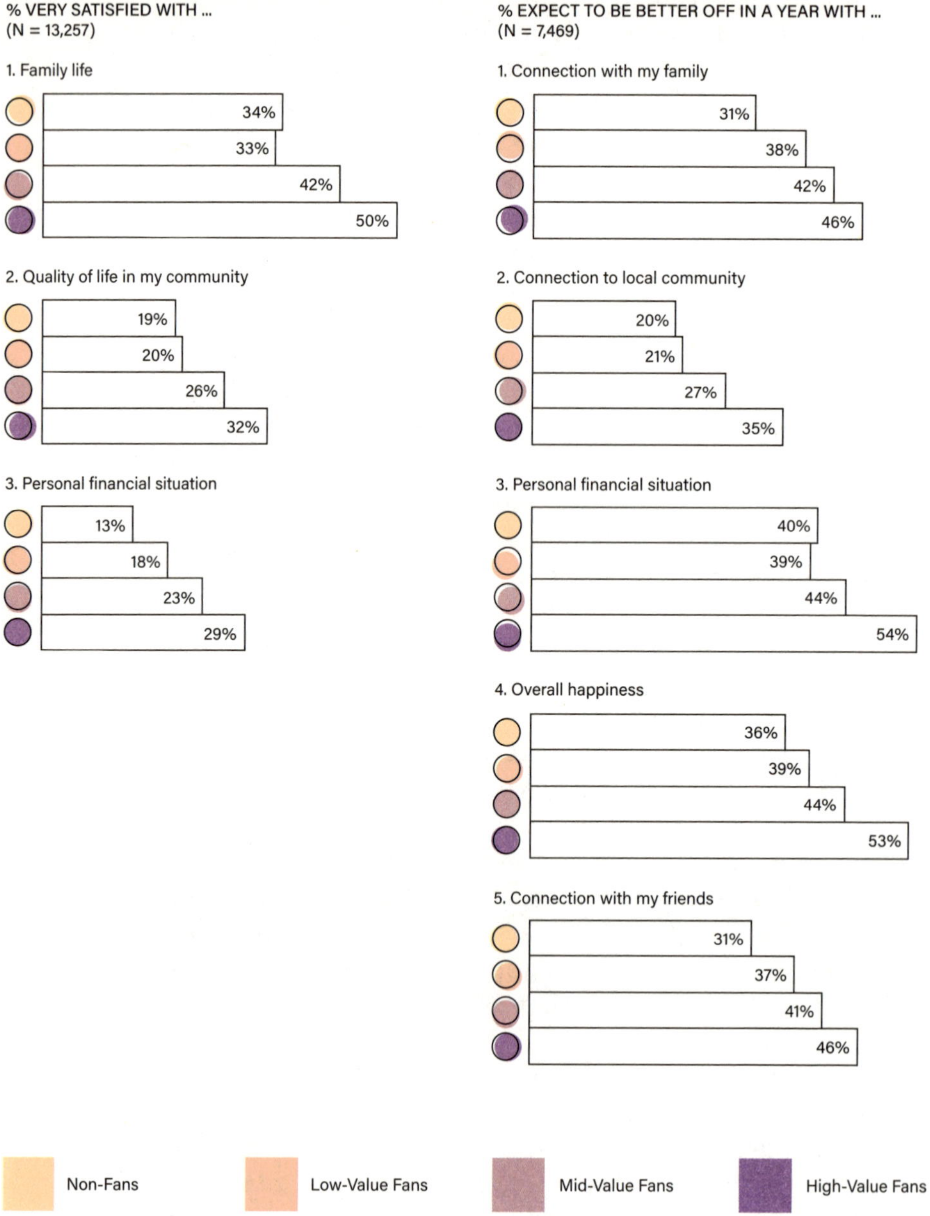

% VERY SATISFIED WITH ...
(N = 13,257)

1. Family life

- Non-Fans: 34%
- Low-Value Fans: 33%
- Mid-Value Fans: 42%
- High-Value Fans: 50%

2. Quality of life in my community

- Non-Fans: 19%
- Low-Value Fans: 20%
- Mid-Value Fans: 26%
- High-Value Fans: 32%

3. Personal financial situation

- Non-Fans: 13%
- Low-Value Fans: 18%
- Mid-Value Fans: 23%
- High-Value Fans: 29%

% EXPECT TO BE BETTER OFF IN A YEAR WITH ...
(N = 7,469)

1. Connection with my family

- Non-Fans: 31%
- Low-Value Fans: 38%
- Mid-Value Fans: 42%
- High-Value Fans: 46%

2. Connection to local community

- Non-Fans: 20%
- Low-Value Fans: 21%
- Mid-Value Fans: 27%
- High-Value Fans: 35%

3. Personal financial situation

- Non-Fans: 40%
- Low-Value Fans: 39%
- Mid-Value Fans: 44%
- High-Value Fans: 54%

4. Overall happiness

- Non-Fans: 36%
- Low-Value Fans: 39%
- Mid-Value Fans: 44%
- High-Value Fans: 53%

5. Connection with my friends

- Non-Fans: 31%
- Low-Value Fans: 37%
- Mid-Value Fans: 41%
- High-Value Fans: 46%

Legend: Non-Fans | Low-Value Fans | Mid-Value Fans | High-Value Fans

3.10 **The percent who are very satisfied with and who expect to be better off a year from now.**
Q1: On the whole, how satisfied are you with the following aspects of your life?
Q2: Do you feel that a year from now you will be better off, just about the same, or worse off?

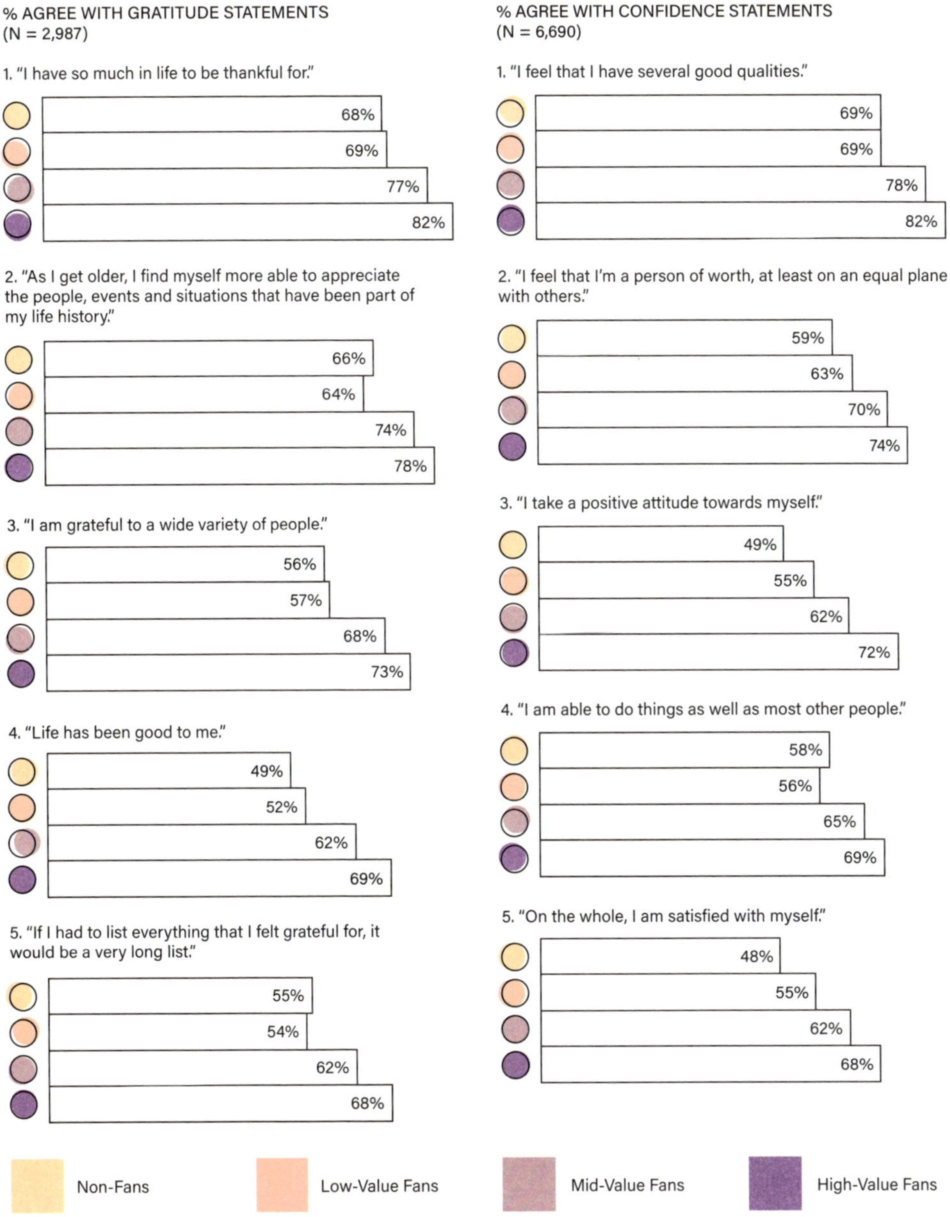

% AGREE WITH GRATITUDE STATEMENTS
(N = 2,987)

1. "I have so much in life to be thankful for."
- Non-Fans: 68%
- Low-Value Fans: 69%
- Mid-Value Fans: 77%
- High-Value Fans: 82%

2. "As I get older, I find myself more able to appreciate the people, events and situations that have been part of my life history."
- Non-Fans: 66%
- Low-Value Fans: 64%
- Mid-Value Fans: 74%
- High-Value Fans: 78%

3. "I am grateful to a wide variety of people."
- Non-Fans: 56%
- Low-Value Fans: 57%
- Mid-Value Fans: 68%
- High-Value Fans: 73%

4. "Life has been good to me."
- Non-Fans: 49%
- Low-Value Fans: 52%
- Mid-Value Fans: 62%
- High-Value Fans: 69%

5. "If I had to list everything that I felt grateful for, it would be a very long list."
- Non-Fans: 55%
- Low-Value Fans: 54%
- Mid-Value Fans: 62%
- High-Value Fans: 68%

% AGREE WITH CONFIDENCE STATEMENTS
(N = 6,690)

1. "I feel that I have several good qualities."
- Non-Fans: 69%
- Low-Value Fans: 69%
- Mid-Value Fans: 78%
- High-Value Fans: 82%

2. "I feel that I'm a person of worth, at least on an equal plane with others."
- Non-Fans: 59%
- Low-Value Fans: 63%
- Mid-Value Fans: 70%
- High-Value Fans: 74%

3. "I take a positive attitude towards myself."
- Non-Fans: 49%
- Low-Value Fans: 55%
- Mid-Value Fans: 62%
- High-Value Fans: 72%

4. "I am able to do things as well as most other people."
- Non-Fans: 58%
- Low-Value Fans: 56%
- Mid-Value Fans: 65%
- High-Value Fans: 69%

5. "On the whole, I am satisfied with myself."
- Non-Fans: 48%
- Low-Value Fans: 55%
- Mid-Value Fans: 62%
- High-Value Fans: 68%

Legend: Non-Fans | Low-Value Fans | Mid-Value Fans | High-Value Fans

3.11 The percent who agree with gratitude and confidence statements.
Q1 (Gratitude): How much do you agree with the following statements about your life?
Q2 (Confidence): How much do you agree wth each of the following statements about yourself?

aspects of their lives would look a year out. These included overall happiness, personal finances, connection with family, connection with friends, and connection with the local community. As you can see in Figure 3.10, a familiar pattern emerges: The bigger the fan, the more optimistic about the future, across all aspects of life.

Interestingly, High-Value Fans are much more optimistic than lower-value fans about their connection to their local communities. Seeing this, we wondered if loyalty to a local team might drive this connection. But we found no evidence to suggest this. The connection is not driven by an attachment to a local team or that team's relative success. Rather, the fans' greater number of social interactions forges stronger bonds with their local communities.

Fig. 3.11

As an additional measure of wellbeing, we used The Gratitude Questionnaire, which was developed to measure people's experience of, well, gratitude.[12] As the next chart indicates, the bigger the fan, the higher the degree of gratitude, across the board.

Fig. 3.11

Finally, it occurred to us that people with robust social networks, and with elevated levels of happiness, satisfaction, optimism, and gratitude, might also move through the world with more confidence. To measure confidence and self-worth among fans, we borrowed attributes from the Rosenberg Self-Esteem Scale, the instrument most used to measure self-regard.[13] We see, once again, that High-Value Fans outpace all other segments.

This is the fandom flywheel in action. Propelled by its feedback loop, the flywheel spins ever faster with each added activity, not only pulling fans deeper into their engagement with sports, but also producing greater social connectedness, which generates an elevated sense of wellbeing among fans.

When we remove our preconceived notions, connect the dots, and understand the logic that underpins fandom, the connections between fan activities and heightened wellbeing become clear. And as we'll see in Chapter 4, when leveraged mindfully, that sense of wellbeing can grow beyond individual fans' lives, positively impacting entire communities.

04 The Benefits of Belonging

At the beginning of his tenure as the 19th Surgeon General of the United States, Dr. Vivek Murthy took a "listening tour" throughout the country.

"We were welcomed into communities from Alabama to North Carolina, from California to Indiana," he recalls in his 2020 book, *Together: The Healing Power of Human Connection in a Sometimes Lonely World*.[14] "We sat down in small group meetings and large town halls, spending time with parents, teachers, pastors, small business owners, philanthropists, and community leaders. Everywhere we went, we asked a simple question: How can we help?"

Many of these discussions confirmed suspected pain points: obesity, heart disease, diabetes, and opioid addiction. But one recurring theme surprised Dr. Murthy: "Loneliness ran like a dark thread through many of the more obvious issues that people brought to my attention."

Research confirms Dr. Murthy's observation about the underlying condition of loneliness. "If you are lonely," writes Noreena Hertz in her 2021 book, *The Lonely Century: How to Restore Human Connection in a World That's Pulling Apart*, "in addition to being at greater risk for mental health issues such as depression and anxiety, you have a 29% higher risk of coronary heart disease, a 32% higher risk of stroke, and a 64% higher risk of developing clinical dementia. If you feel lonely or are socially isolated, you are almost 30% more likely to die prematurely than if you are not."[15]

How is it possible that something we think of as an emotional condition can have such a poisonous physiological impact? As it turns out, loneliness is a stressor that triggers hormonal responses in the body. Over time, those stress hormones can contribute to dangerous physical maladies.

Fortunately, loneliness has an antidote in its polar opposite: belonging. "While loneliness has the potential to kill, belonging has even more potential to heal," Dr. Murthy contends. In his role as Surgeon General and in treating patients, he notes, "I met thousands of people who struggled with addiction to opioids, alcohol, and other substances, and when I reflect on those who made it through that dark tunnel and emerged in recovery, nearly all of them described a trusted relationship or trusted group of close family or friends who had made their recovery possible."

Research shows that belonging also enhances physical wellness. *National Geographic* Fellow Dan Buettner, author of *The Blue Zones: Lessons for Living Longer from the People Who've Lived the Longest*,[16] has spent his career studying "blue zones": geographic regions known for statistically higher-than-normal life expectancy. Healthy diet and regular exercise are, unsurprisingly, shared attributes across these blue zones. But when we sat down with Buettner to discuss the health impacts of social connection, he told us, "If you don't have three friends you can count on on a bad day, it shaves about eight years off your life expectancy, as opposed to somebody who's well connected."

Buettner first recognized the health benefits of socialization while conducting research on the blue zone of Okinawa, Japan, where he encountered the "ritualized vehicle for companionship" called moai. In *The Blue Zones*, first published in 2008, he explains, "The notion of moai — which roughly means 'meeting for a common purpose' originated as a means of a village's financial support system [...] Today the idea has expanded to become more of a social support network."

The first moai Buettner witnessed consisted of five women, ages 77 to 102, who gathered daily to gossip, laugh, problem-solve, and commiserate. It occurred to him that "Japanese women on average were doing something special to live almost eight percent longer than American women. Their moai might very well be part of the equation. Chronic stress takes its toll on overall health, and these women have a culturally ingrained mechanism that sheds it every afternoon at 3:30 p.m."

More than a decade after this first observation, Buettner reflects, "Most of the things that are implanted in the American brain when it comes to things that favor longevity are things that are relentlessly marketed to us, like super foods and supplements, but I would argue there's better research for the impact of long-term social connectivity than there is for any diet or any supplement or any quote unquote superfood."

You can see why, though Dr. Murthy had "never considered [loneliness] as a potential public health priority," he now recognizes that "overcoming loneliness and building a more connected future is an urgent mission that we can and must tackle together." We could not agree more with the Surgeon General. But how can we improve our collective sense of belonging? How can we foster life-changing social connections, at scale?

Coincidentally, at the same time the loneliness problem began receiving mainstream attention across the US, we were on our own journey into the social lives of sports fans. The relationship between the two phenomena became obvious: Fandom creates belonging, and belonging is the antidote to loneliness.

UNDERSTANDING LONELINESS

Before we talk about fandom as an antidote to loneliness, we need to break down the loneliness problem in more detail.

The word "lonely" may conjure up images of a person physically isolated from others — an elderly woman sitting alone at her dinner table, or a child sequestered in the school library while his classmates are on the playground. However, one can be alone without feeling lonely, and one can feel lonely while surrounded by people. In other words, whether you feel lonely or not is not about your proximity to other people; it's about your connection to them, or lack thereof. As Dr. Murthy puts it, "What's missing when you're lonely is the feeling of closeness, trust, and the affection of genuine friends, loved ones, and community." Loneliness is effectively the absence of meaningful social connection. To be connected is to be seen and heard and supported by others. To be lonely is to be bereft of affection, intimacy, and fellowship with others.

It's also important to note that loneliness — like belonging — can manifest across different dimensions. Drawing on a broad body of academic work, Dr. Murthy points to three specific types of relationships that are important: intimate, as in a close confidante or life partner; relational, as in connections to a circle of friends; and collective, as in a sense of belonging to a larger community. Noreena Hertz argues that people can also feel connected or disconnected in a fourth dimension: at the societal level. People may lack support not only in familial or social contexts, she notes, but also feel politically and/or economically excluded." Both Murthy and Hertz agree that a person can experience connection in one or more of these areas while experiencing disconnection — or loneliness — in others. For instance, a happily married person might feel loneliness if he lacks the companionship of friends, or a person who has an active friend circle might feel lonely if she doesn't have a close confidante.

To address the multidimensional crisis of loneliness, we need multidimensional solutions: tools that enable people to connect with one another in meaningful ways, to feel part of something larger than themselves, and to navigate challenging social circumstances. To illustrate how fandom can solve for loneliness, we'd like to introduce you to Jennifer Pratt, who has experienced fandom as the glue that holds her family together; as the bonding agent that connects strangers and turns them into friends; and as the key to developing a sense of belonging.

IT ALL STARTED WITH A JERSEY

As is the case for so many fans, Jennifer's fandom began with family. She first encountered the NFL as a ten-year-old in 1991, when she travelled to visit relatives in Los Angeles from her home in Kingston, Jamaica. "My uncles took me to a Raider game, and that is where my mind was blown," she told us. "I was like, 'What is this?' You don't have professional sports like that in Jamaica. That energy … I'll never forget that feeling of being at a football game. It's like getting shocked — an electric shock — but instead of my body, it was my spirit."

A year later, Jennifer immigrated to the United States, where her family kept alive the Jamaican tradition of Sunday dinners, but with a distinctly American twist: NFL games as the centerpiece. "I have a very large family, seventeen uncles and two aunts. Football was where we came together. It was this unifying family thing we did, where I could hang out with my uncles, and I got this cohesive family time." While the women in her family gathered in the kitchen and the rest of the kids played together outside, Jennifer stayed focused on the game with her uncles. "I would just sit there, watching the screen. I didn't know what was going on, but I liked it."

Eventually, two uncles — Andrew and Stephen — taught Jennifer the rules of the game (and how to throw a perfect spiral). "They are the ones who would explain things to me and guide me through it, without making me feel stupid, which I appreciated. My Uncle Andrew got me my first Raider jersey from a swap meet. I still have that jersey."

Looking back, Jennifer believes that football helped her find her place in the family. Her bond with her uncles remains strong today, held together by three decades of shared fandom. "There are forty women in my family, but I am the only one who will watch sports with the guys, she said. "It's why I get along with my uncles so much."

Today Jennifer is a highly intelligent, compassionate, outspoken woman with a wicked sense of humor. She's a special-needs educator and business owner. From her half-blonde braids, to her six-foot-tall frame, to her boisterous personality, Jennifer commands attention when she walks into a room. So, when she told us, "I was a shy kid. Very shy," we found that hard to imagine. She explained: "I was an immigrant in this country. I came from a very small island, and now I'm this Black kid around a bunch of white kids who all speak differently than I do. They don't understand me, we have different customs and cultures. So, I didn't feel good about myself. I was the weird Jamaican kid with the funky accent. I was the only Black kid, and that's a very polarizing feeling to be the other, which is literally what I was called: 'the other.' I hated school. I was good at school, but I didn't love being there because I got picked on. My family was my refuge, and in that refuge was Sunday dinners, and as I hung out with my uncles more, a little confidence bubble started to grow."

At the age of eleven, Jennifer's newfound love for football, her acceptance among her uncles, and her ability to connect "as one of the guys" helped establish some much-needed self-confidence. In fact, Jennifer believes her fandom — and the resulting relationships — helped her find her voice. "Middle school was where the bullying for my accent started. That's also when guys and girls started hooking up, and I was a short, fat kid. No one was interested in me. All I had was football. I needed some friends, so I saw some kids wearing jerseys, and I was like, 'You like football?' They were like, 'Dude, we love football.' 'Who's your team?' This one kid, Raymond, was like, 'The Raiders,' and I was like, 'You're my people. I hang out with you now.' So, I followed these dudes around, and they were like, 'Why is she here?' They weren't nice to me, really, but they let me sit with them, and that's all I wanted: someone to let me sit with them, because I was tired of sitting by myself."

Fandom enabled Jennifer to take the first step on the road to belonging, but it wasn't a panacea. "When I got to high school, kids were super mean — like beat me up to the point that I was in the hospital mean. But Raymond came to see me in the hospital. He brought me flowers. He spray-painted them Raiders' colors. Raymond's dad was a Raider fan, so I was like, 'You guys want to come to Sunday dinner?'" That invitation built a bridge to a lifelong friendship. "Raymond is still around today," Jennifer said. "We go to games together. He's like family. And it all started with a jersey."

During high school, the tide started to turn for Jennifer. She began standing up for herself and others. "There was this guy named Eric," she told us. "He would grab girls' butts. The girls wouldn't say anything. So, I saw Eric do that, and I was like *Smack!* 'Don't do that!' He flew back, shocked. He looked at me like, 'That's the girl who fights,' and I was like, 'No, that's the girl who stands up for herself and other people.' I didn't see him grab another butt after that."

Jennifer traces this transformation — from shy immigrant kid to girl who stands up to the boys — back to sports fandom: "I always knew I had a voice, but I felt afraid when I first moved here. The older I got, that part of me that was afraid just didn't exist anymore. I don't know that if I hadn't hung out with my uncles that I would have discovered that. Without knowing it, indirectly they gave me the chance to be myself and to have the space where it was okay to just be me, without fear or reservation, or ever even thinking about how someone would perceive me."

As it turns out, her uncles helped to plant two seeds for Jennifer: her love for football and her awareness of fandom's ability to help her navigate loneliness, bigotry, and bullying. Today, she actively leverages her fandom to deepen relationships, energize her social life, and build community.

Jennifer is far from alone in reaping these benefits of fandom. We have already established that sports fans — especially High-Value Fans — not only have more friends, but also engage with their social circles far more often. It would follow, then, that fans would experience more belonging. To test this hypothesis, we integrated the UCLA Loneliness Scale, the gold standard for loneliness measurement, into our surveys.[17] As you'll see in the next chart, the differences are stark.

Once again, we see the fandom flywheel at work. The difference between Non-Fans and High-Value Fans is dramatic. For instance, 61% percent of High-Value Fans strongly agree that they "feel close to people," compared to just 37% of Non-Fans. How is it possible that fandom elevates a fan's sense of belonging in this way?

Fig. 4.1

We believe the answer is scale. Because sports are ubiquitous in our culture, fandom gives people the ability to strike up a conversation with nearly anyone, nearly anywhere. Fandom is easily signaled: by something as simple as an emblem on a baseball cap, a sticker on a laptop, or a license-plate rim. Further, fandom gives people hundreds of opportunities a year to host a watch party, connect with a friend over a beer, or jump into a group chat with family members in multiple time zones. Engaging in sports fandom increases our opportunities to make multidimensional

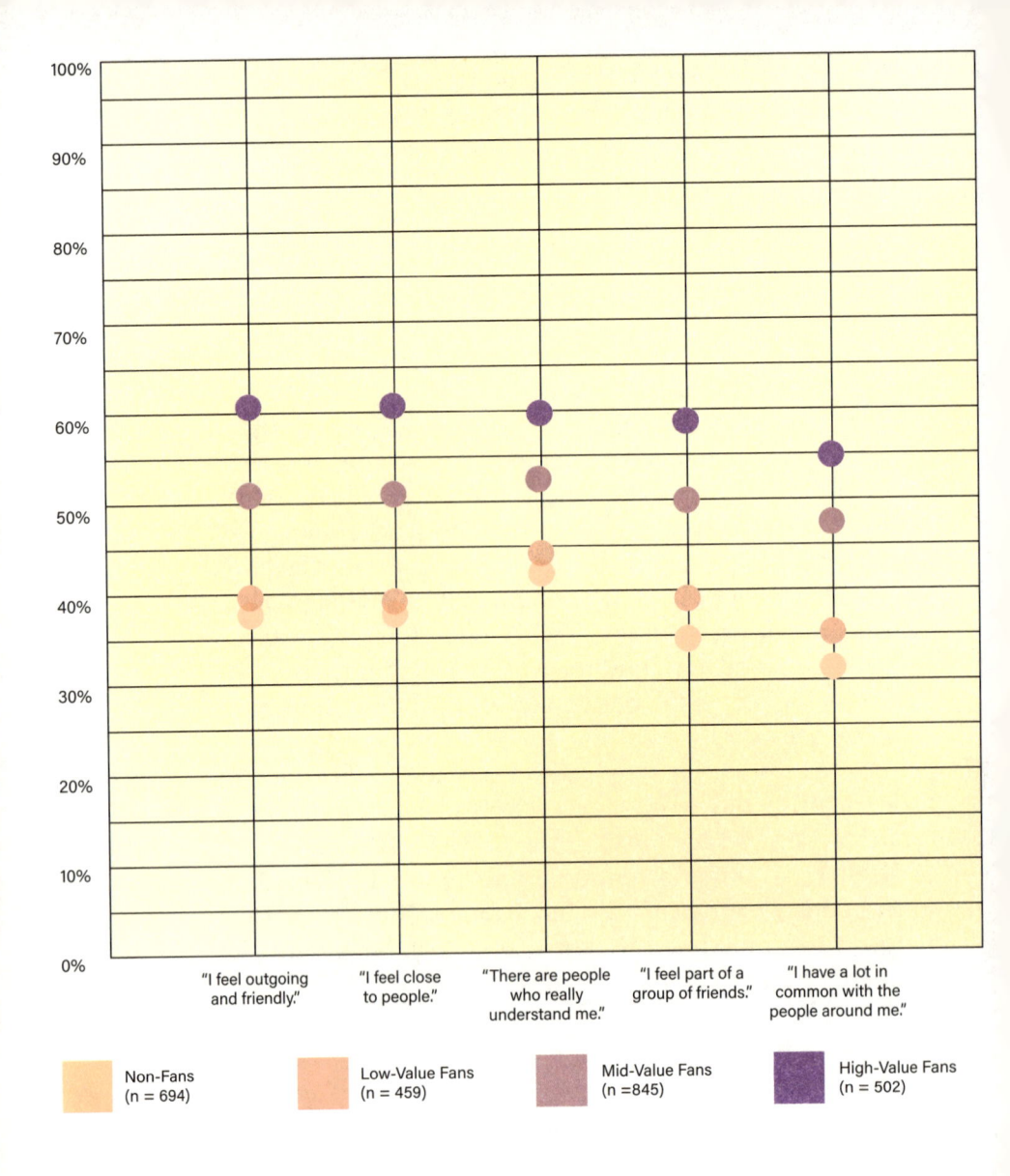

4.1 The percent who agree with statements from UCLA Loneliness Scale. N = 2,500.
Q: How much do you agree with each of the following statements about yourself? Please read each statement carefully.

Statement	Non-Fans (n = 694)	Low-Value Fans (n = 459)	Mid-Value Fans (n = 845)	High-Value Fans (n = 502)
"I feel outgoing and friendly."	38%	40%	52%	62%
"I feel close to people."	39%	40%	52%	62%
"There are people who really understand me."	43%	45%	54%	61%
"I feel part of a group of friends."	36%	40%	51%	60%
"I have a lot in common with the people around me."	33%	37%	49%	57%

THE BENEFITS OF BELONGING

social connections, which encourages deeper engagement in fandom, which only begets more social connection. Over time, this feedback loop makes a dramatic impact on our day-to-day lives. At the end of the day, the more one activates the social power of their fandom, the more they reap the benefits.

Fans like Jennifer are not one bit surprised when presented with the evidence that fandom is a social superconductor. As she says, "Intrinsically, all humans need and want connections. How do you go about that? For me it's football."

FAST FRIENDS

As we've discovered, fans have more friends. They interact more often. And, on balance, they feel more connected. Those facts aren't just something that's nice to know. Writ large, they signal fandom's immense potential to impact society.

Being a fan creates a greater sense of belonging, and belonging is something that we desperately need. In 2020, a Cigna survey of more than 10,000 adults revealed that three in five Americans (61%) are lonely.[18] Notably, that research was conducted before the COVID-19 pandemic upended our social lives. The structural factors — economic, technological, cultural — contributing to isolation were in place well before COVID-19. We're just beginning to understand the effects of the extended period of pandemic-induced social isolation. Thanks in part to authors like Murthy and Hertz, the "loneliness epidemic" is top of mind now. Beyond merely understanding its causes, we feel called to activate solutions. We believe sports is one of them.

The magnitude of the loneliness problem is daunting. Undoubtedly, a comprehensive solution will require systemic changes the scale of which are difficult to imagine. But we don't need to wait for that to happen. Fandom is a powerful antidote to loneliness, and one that we can activate, at scale, right now. Together, fans can use sports to expand social connection, develop a sense of belonging for themselves, and offer that sense of belonging to others. In fact, if you're sports fan, whether you're conscious of it or not, you might already be using sports this way. Jennifer certainly has.

In her early thirties, when Jennifer temporarily relocated to Denver, Colorado, she didn't know a soul in town. So, she activated fandom's superpower: She went to the nearest sports bar, knowing she'd find someone to talk to there. Jennifer calls these casual acquaintances "fast friends." She explains, "All of a sudden, you're sitting next to someone, and you're like, 'You like this sport? Cool. Now we're buddies for two hours.' You may never see that person again in your life, but for two hours you were best friends because you were rooting for the same team."

These experiences are ubiquitous among sports fans: No matter where you land, if you can find a bar with a game on, you can find someone to talk to, and you can turn that room into a space where you belong. In Denver, Jennifer transformed some of those fast friendships into lifelong relationships: "My core group of friends were people I met at the bar. I was just welcomed into this group. People started inviting me into their houses for games. So, I was like, 'Can I cook for you? I can flex my Jamaican culinary skills.'" And then she turned around and opened the door to others. "Football became the thing that helped me pick up little orphan friends, where it's like, 'Oh, you don't have a family? Come be part of my football family.' That's one of the things that the NFL looks like to me: It's like a big old melting pot."

Research suggests that even fleeting "fast friend" conversations between people — for five minutes or even five seconds — can elevate a person's sense of wellbeing. In his 2021 book, *The Power of*

Strangers: The Benefits of Connecting in a Suspicious World, journalist Joe Keohane examines both our hesitance and our need to connect, however briefly, with people we don't know.[19]

Keohane contends that "the single best predictor of happiness and wellbeing is the quality of a person's social relationships." He notes, however, that most studies focus on "close relationships: family, friends, coworkers." What about that other dimension of belonging: a sense of connection to a larger community? He turns to the work of psychologists Gillian Sandstrom and Elizabeth Dunn, who have studied the impact of what are known in psychology as "minimal social interactions." Even something as simple as talking to your barista while waiting for your triple shot latte, they found, can result in "a stronger sense of belonging and an improved mood" (even before the caffeine kicks in).[20]

In a subsequent study, Sandstrom and Dunn looked at "weak ties": a social category that describes "a passing acquaintance, or people we know by sight who aren't necessarily friends."[21] They sent 58 college students out into the world, instructing them to tally the number of interactions they had with both weak ties and "strong ties," like close friends and family members. The results? "[T]he people who had more interactions with weak ties ... were happier and felt a greater sense of belonging than those who had fewer." Additionally, the students reported greater happiness "on days they had more weak-tie interactions." To test their results, Sandstrom and Dunn ran the study again, this time with non-students. In the end, both studies confirmed that "interactions with weak ties were more potent on days when participants had fewer overall interactions." In other words, "minimal social interactions" with "fast friends" matter. A lot.

How can something as seemingly insignificant as small talk at a bus stop or the grocery checkout change our lives? According to Sandstrom and Dunn, "Weak-tie relationships give us short, low-cost, informal interactions, which often provide new information and social variety. As a result, we are often pleasantly surprised by these moments."

It seems that these minimal interactions have a flywheel of their own. It takes some effort to get a "talking to strangers" habit moving, but once the positive feedback loop kicks in, the benefits might surprise you. Not only can a pleasant conversation with a stranger put a smile on your face, it can trigger an uptick in oxytocin, also known as the "bonding" hormone. That jolt of oxytocin kicks off a "cascade of hormones and neurotransmitters" that ultimately alters brain activity "and makes you feel happy." Imagine the ripple effect if every sports fan committed to engaging in one positive conversation with a stranger every day. Next time you see someone signaling their fandom, consider it an opportunity to say hello.

But what about the more lasting, strong-tie relationships Dan Buettner observed in the moais of Okinawa? Can fandom help us formulate those?

After studying existing blue zones across the globe, Buettner turned his attention to creating new ones through Blue Zone Projects, an initiative that partners with municipalities to elevate the wellness of their citizens. Integral to this process is the intentional formation of moais: connecting small groups of people based on "interests, values, demography, and geography," and then engineering "the first ten or so meetings." After that, "60 to 70% of people who take the time to join our moais stay with our moais." Why? The combination of shared interests and propinquity — time spent together — foments friendships that extend beyond their original boundaries. So, over time, the people you met at the potluck moai or the walking moai become the people you call when you're celebrating a milestone moment, when you need emotional support, or when they do.

When we first read about moais we thought, *There it is! That's what fandom does! That's what we've been observing for years!* We asked Buettner, a non-fan who jokingly admits his knowledge of basketball amounts to "it involves a ball," if he saw the parallel. "When you think about fans," he told us, "You're going to share the interest in sports, you'll share proximity because you're showing up to the game, you have this ready-made opportunity for people to meet, so you have an environment really ripe for creating moais." Thanks to the frequency built into sports, Buettner posits that fans are more likely "to hit that tipping point" where friendships grow beyond their origin points, and "connect in the real world, which is where the magic happens." Qualitatively, we have seen this proved true time and again: a connection that begins at the sports bar, in an arena, or through a fantasy league grows beyond its origin point into a sustained and sustaining friendship.

FANDOM'S FLEXIBILITY

The multidimensional nature of loneliness should not be overlooked. As we pointed out earlier, loneliness — and belonging — exist across different dimensions. People thrive when they have intimate relationships, familial relationships, connection to a community, and a feeling that they have a place in society. The problem of loneliness is so pernicious precisely because it can manifest across these different dimensions, where a single person can experience connection on one dimension and disconnection on another. Attempting to find solutions to a multidimensional problem like loneliness can feel like a never-ending game of whack-a-mole.

We contend that fandom can be part of the solution because fandom has the flexibility to suit different social contexts, enabling connection on multiple levels. For example, fandom can facilitate wholehearted, lasting friendships of the moai variety, as well as the sort of "weak-tie," "fast friendships" that deepen one's connection to a local community. This ability to answer the call no matter the social context is fandom's most important attribute. It simply requires fans to create belonging for themselves and share that belonging with others.

Fandom's ability to make connections certainly aligns with the average fan's experience. As we have shared our findings with friends and strangers alike, we continually hear heartwarming testimonials of fandom's social power, a flickering recognition of a deep truth. Naturally, these stories exist at a person-to-person level. But does the power of fandom extend to the societal level? As you will see in the following two chapters, fandom has the potential to soften the harder edges of the polarization problem that plagues society today.

05 The Polarization Problem

Once we identified fandom as a bridge out of loneliness and into belonging, we started to think bigger. How might fandom — and fandom's benefits — intersect with other spheres of life? How and where does fandom interact with issues bubbling to the surface in our larger culture? We began exploring this question early in 2020, as crisis-level social issues transitioned from a steady simmer to a rolling boil.

Before we dig in, though, let's set the sociopolitical stage. If you follow American news even passively, not a day goes by where you don't see some evidence of our country's deeply ingrained social divisions. Our citizenry has retreated into ideological camps that vehemently disagree about — well, everything: fundamental values, lifestyle decisions, and what counts as "true." Wildly opposing belief systems aren't the only features separating these camps. We are, in fact, distancing ourselves from one another geographically, too, withdrawing into like-minded neighborhoods and community groups.

How did we get here?

Well, our tendency to "sort" makes sense from a psychological perspective. It's human nature to want to feel safe, like we belong. We seek that sense of belonging from people who share our values and ideologies. The problem arises when "sorting" isolates us from anyone outside our ideological camps. As Bill Bishop says in his 2008 book *The Big Sort: Why the Clustering of Like-Minded America is Pulling Us Apart*, "like-minded, homogeneous groups squelch dissent, grow more extreme in their thinking, and ignore evidence that their positions are wrong."[22] Sound familiar? The more distant sorted groups become from one another, the less human they seem to each other.

Unfortunately, this describes the US, socially and politically. But it wasn't always like this. According to Ezra Klein, author of *Why We're Polarized*, in the mid-twentieth century, political parties were far more heterogeneous than they are today.[23] It might be hard to imagine from where we stand now, but back then we had liberal Democrats, Southern conservative Democrats, traditional conservative Republicans, and liberal Republicans. During that era, Klein contends, the two parties were "coalitions that looked alike, lived similar lives, and thought only somewhat differently." In other words, while members of opposing parties may have differed on certain policy opinions, they shared important similarities, too, enough to maintain their humanity in each other's eyes.

Not so today. As Klein describes it, the political parties have transformed into "two warring camps that look different, live different lives in different places, and find themselves in ever deeper disagreement." In fact, demographic, political, and cultural sorting have aligned such that the categories "Democrat" and "Republican" have become what Klein calls "mega-identities": a cluster of seemingly unrelated traits that "fuse together into a single sense of self." Even the most casual observer of social dynamics knows the identity categories "white," "rural," and "evangelical" track Republican, and "non-white," "urban," and "non-religious" track Democrat. Additionally, we know which parts of the US map skew Blue and which Red.

But it doesn't stop there. Today, membership in a political party signals allegiance to a whole host of identity categories, beliefs, and personal choices. For example, Klein offers, "living in a city, being a liberal, shopping at Trader Joe's, and dabbling in Zen meditation may not have much to do with one another in terms of public policy, but they reinforce a singular identity." The same goes for living in the country, being a conservative, shopping at Walmart, and attending Bible study on Thursday nights. These days, it seems, nearly every choice we make indicates

— intentionally or not, accurately or not — some sort of in-group status. In a highly sorted social landscape, whether you drive a Toyota Prius or a Ford F-150, or whether you buy organic or conventional vegetables implies membership in one group and opposition to the other.

Lilliana Mason, in her 2018 book, *Uncivil Agreement: How Politics Became Our Identity*, argues that these mega-identities are the true source of our polarization problem.[24] She writes: "This is the American identity crisis. Not that we have partisan identities, we've always had those. The crisis emerges when partisan identities fall into alignment with other social identities, stoking our intolerance of each other to levels that are unsupported by our degrees of political disagreement." These divisions have become so entrenched, it's hard to see a way out.

Let's be clear: Group membership — partisan and otherwise — is not *prima facie* negative. In fact, as Mason contends, affiliation is not only an innate psychological drive, but also serves a larger social function. First, "without a sense of social cohesion, we would have a hard time organizing societies and civilizations." Second, she notes, the human brain needs to categorize to understand the world. This process includes categorizing people. Third, the social categories we create allow us to "understand ourselves and our place in the world." She explains, "Once we are part of a group, we know how to identify ourselves in relation to the other people in our society, and we derive an emotional connection and sense of wellbeing from being group members."

Emotional connection and wellbeing sound good, right? Yes. And yet ...

Once we identify with a particular group, due to our tribal nature, we simultaneously "otherize" people outside that group. The more distant an in-group becomes from an out-group, the more likely that "otherizing" will become all-out "dehumanizing." And, as history has taught us, dehumanization is the first step to turning perceived "others" into mortal enemies.

Studies have shown that opposing group members "treat each other with bias and even prejudice," writes Mason, a dynamic that heightens when two groups are pitted in — or perceive themselves to be pitted in — competition. Then it becomes dangerous: A perceived threat, however minor, can cause group members to lose the ability to evaluate objective reality. As Mason cautions, "those who identify with a social group are more likely to take action to defend it," because their individual self-esteem is tied to the group status. The more a member's esteem is wrapped up in the group status, the greater that person's emotional reactivity. This is the breeding ground for the enmity we now experience. Turn on the evening news any day of the week, and you'll see this dynamic in play.

How do you dissolve barriers that separate social groups? How do you get mutually "othered" individuals to meet on common ground? Could fandom help? The answer, at least to that last question, is an unequivocal "yes." While fandom won't solve all our social ills, it does appear to soften the barriers between in- and out-groups in meaningful ways.

At first glance, that hypothesis may seem counterintuitive, contrary to the often-performative, sometimes-pernicious tribalism that some sports fans display. But look closer and you'll see that fandom influences our attitudes and actions in ways that run counter to our political identities. We'll walk you through it.

FANDOM IN THE AGE OF COVID

As news about the outbreak of COVID-19 reached the US in the winter of 2020, we saw the toxicity of polarization on full display. As scientists scrambled to understand the rapidly spreading virus, hospitals struggled with an onslaught of gravely ill patients and a shortage of essential equipment and supplies. Meanwhile, the public was thrown into a roiling sea of fear and uncertainty, contradictory information, and conflicting advice. In an already divided populous, the pandemic quickly became not simply a grave public health problem to be addressed and solved as a country, but another battle ground for warring factions. To quarantine or not to quarantine? To mask or not to mask? And later, to vaccinate or not to vaccinate? Answers to these questions signaled allegiance to "us" or "them." This added fuel to an already raging sociopolitical fire.

Meanwhile, by mid-March 2020, the NBA had suspended its regular season, the MLB shuttered spring training, and the NCAA had cancelled March Madness. The circuit board that powered sports fans' social connections had blown, and their whole network went dark. How would fans cope without the social connections sports facilitate? At the same time, the news media was littered with polling data on COVID protocols, showing clear divides between Democrats and Republicans. We wanted to see how the same polling questions would break down among sports fans. Would they respond differently to the COVID crisis?

Fig. 5.1

Driven by relentless curiosity, we added COVID-related questions to our surveys. And we found a clear link between fandom and a willingness to follow COVID protocols. Figure 5.1 shows how seriously respondents took recommendations to stop the spread of COVID, including washing hands frequently, keeping a six-foot "social distance" between themselves and others, and self-quarantining (or remaining "safer at home," in the vernacular of the day). Interestingly, the bigger the fan, the more likely to take these protocols seriously in the moment.

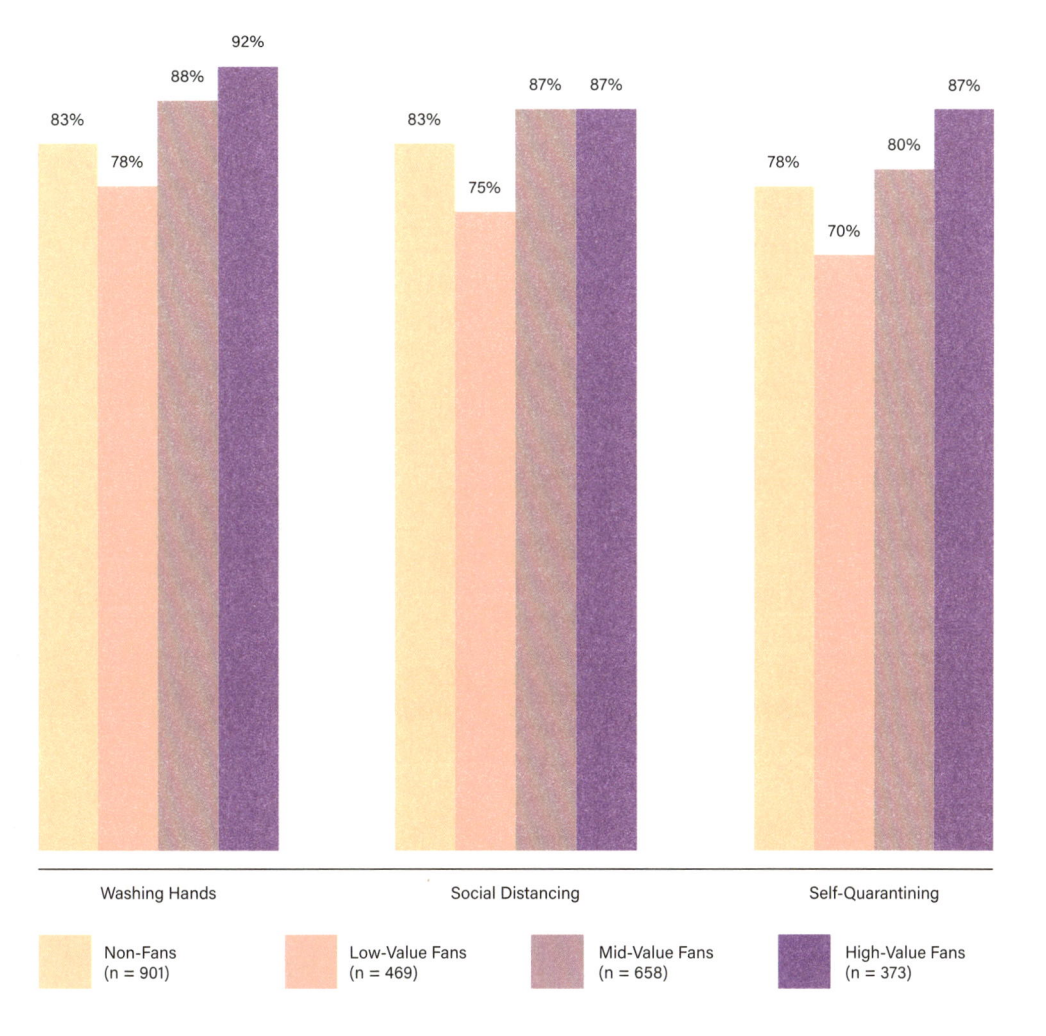

	Washing Hands	Social Distancing	Self-Quarantining
Non-Fans (n = 901)	83%	83%	78%
Low-Value Fans (n = 469)	78%	75%	70%
Mid-Value Fans (n = 658)	88%	87%	80%
High-Value Fans (n = 373)	92%	87%	87%

5.1 **The percent who take COVID-19 measures seriously.** N = 2,401.
Q1: How seriously have you taken the following guidelines for reducing the spread of the coronavirus?
Q2: In November, if the Democratic candidate is Joe Biden and the Republican candidate is Donald Trump, who would you vote for?

These results piqued our curiosity: What could be driving this dynamic? During interviews, we asked respondents why they thought sports fans would be taking these protocols more seriously. A few themes emerged. First, many mentioned the "team" concept that sports promote: You make personal sacrifices for the greater good. Second, they indicated that sports brought to life the severity of the pandemic. When the NBA postponed the season, that signaled the seriousness of COVID. Third, when news broke that NBA players like Rudy Gobert, Donovan Mitchell, and Kevin Durant had contracted COVID, suddenly fans knew people who tested positive — people to whom they felt connected, which brought the pandemic that much closer to them.

There was probably a degree of truth to each of these explanations. But we didn't feel that they told the whole story.

Fig. 5.2

What happens when we look at partisan attitudes through the lens of fandom? We knew that attitudes toward COVID protocols were polarized along party lines. And when we divided fans by political orientation, we did indeed find higher baseline acceptance of COVID protocols among Democrats compared to Republicans. But look at what happens within each party. As illustrated in Figure 5.2, for each measure, we see the subtle impact of fandom, especially among High-Value Fans, who took the measures more seriously than their lower-value ideological peers.

Fig. 5.3

Now, we recognize that our sample sizes for this cut were not terribly robust, so we treated this as a directional finding that needed more validation and exploration. We asked a similar set of questions a few months later in the fall of 2020 — and got the same results.

Was it possible, we wondered, that fandom could influence people's thinking on deeply polarized issues? We continued digging.

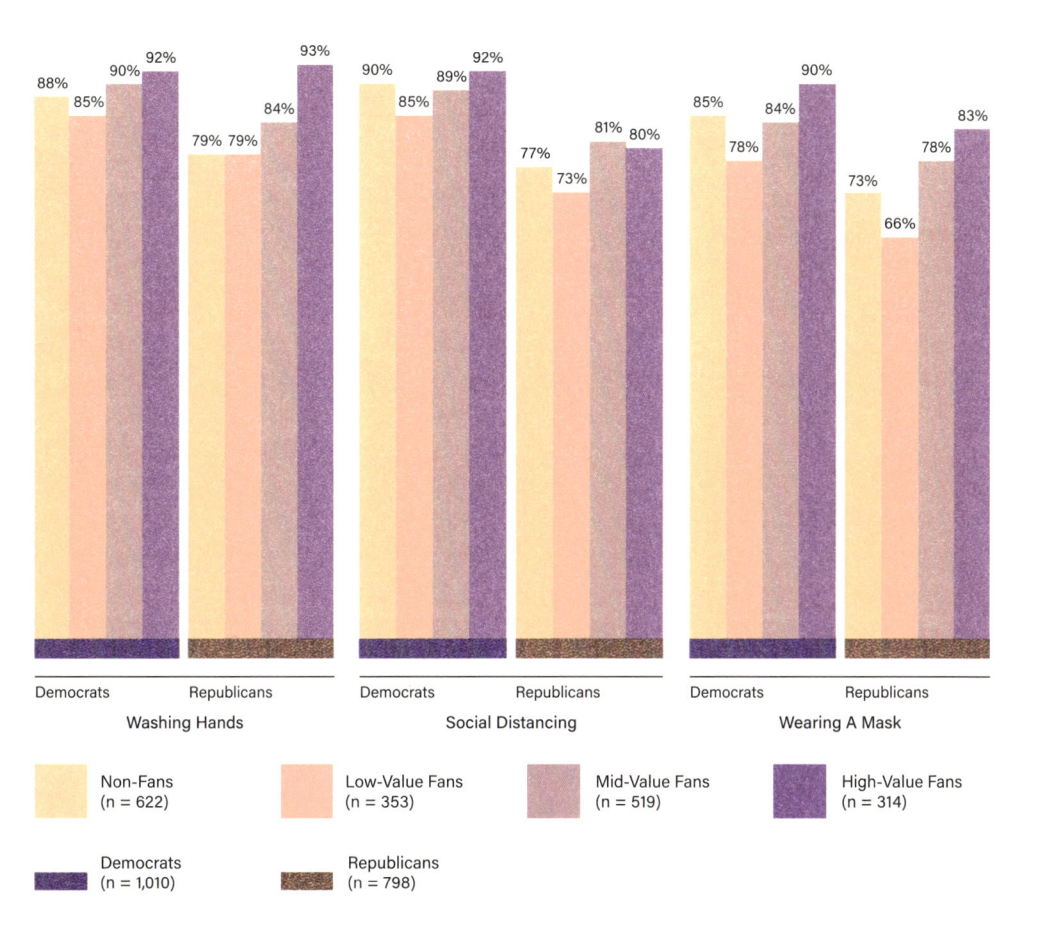

5.2　**The percent who take COVID-19 measures seriously based on party affiliation in April 2020.** N = 1,808. Q: How seriously have you taken the following guidelines for reducing the spread of the coronavirus? Q2: In November, if the Democratic candidate is Joe Biden and the Republican candidate is Donald Trump, who would you vote for?

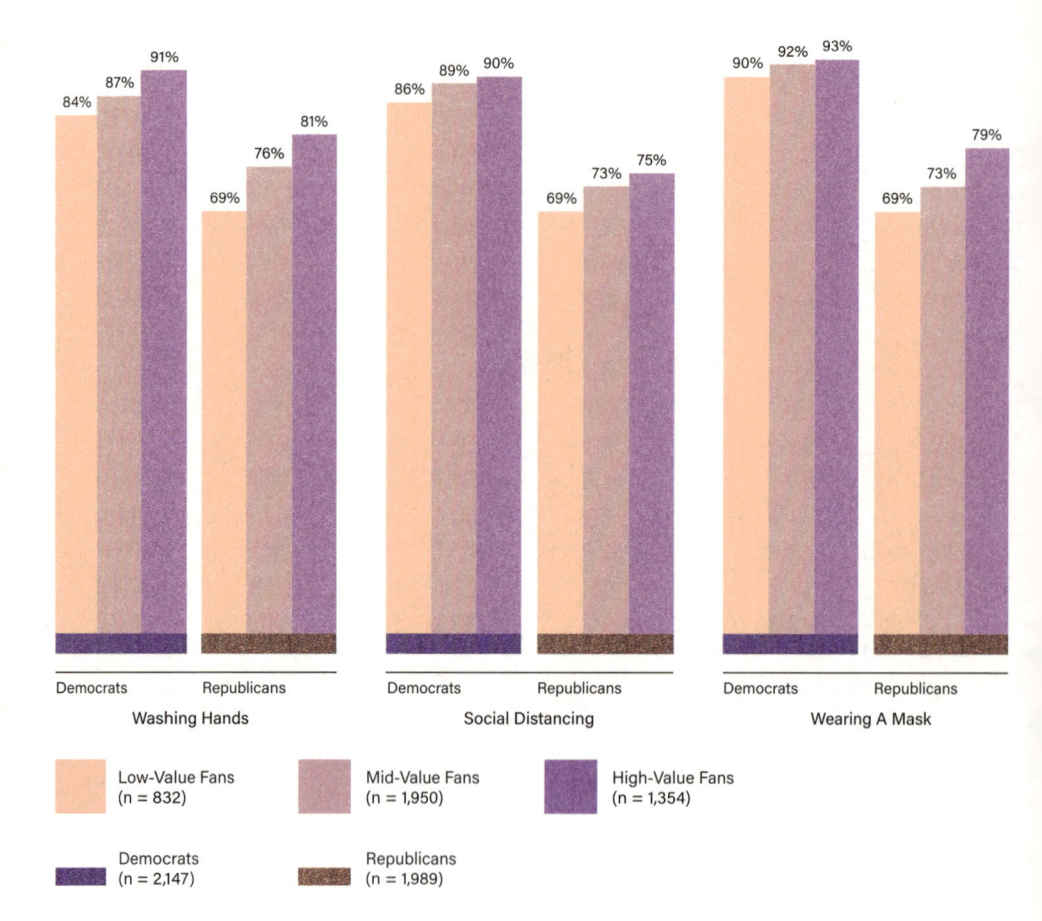

Washing Hands

Democrats: 84%, 87%, 91%
Republicans: 69%, 76%, 81%

Social Distancing

Democrats: 86%, 89%, 90%
Republicans: 69%, 73%, 75%

Wearing A Mask

Democrats: 90%, 92%, 93%
Republicans: 69%, 73%, 79%

Low-Value Fans (n = 832)
Mid-Value Fans (n = 1,950)
High-Value Fans (n = 1,354)
Democrats (n = 2,147)
Republicans (n = 1,989)

5.3 **The percent who take COVID-19 measures seriously based on party affiliation in October 2020.**
N = 4,136.
Q: How seriously have you taken the following guidelines for reducing the spread of the coronavirus?
Q2: In November, if the Democratic candidate is Joe Biden and the Republican candidate is Donald Trump, who would you vote for?

Democrats
(n = 11,513)

- 91% Non-Fans
- 96% Low-Value Fans
- 96% Mid-Value Fans
- 95% High-Value Fans

Republicans
(n = 7,092)

- 53% Non-Fans
- 72% Low-Value Fans
- 75% Mid-Value Fans
- 76% High-Value Fans

Unaffiliated
(n = 5,313)

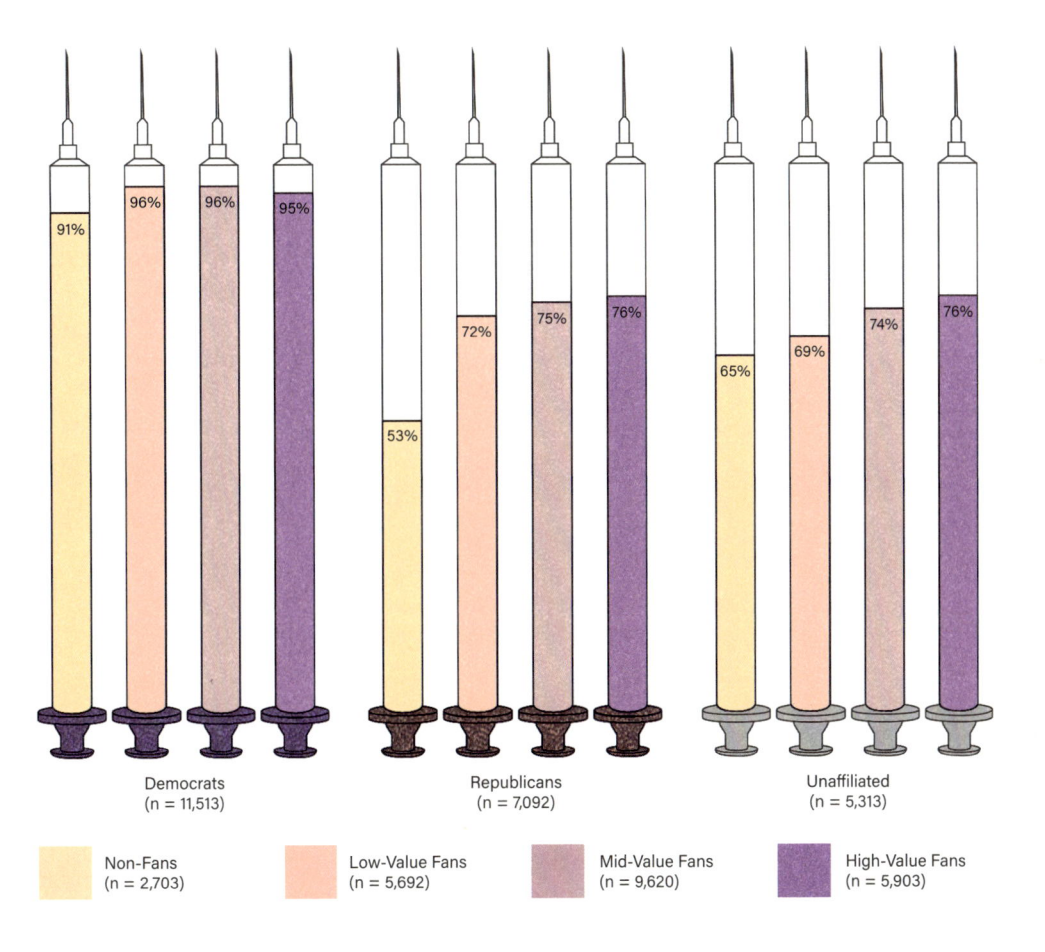

- 65% Non-Fans
- 69% Low-Value Fans
- 74% Mid-Value Fans
- 76% High-Value Fans

Non-Fans (n = 2,703)
Low-Value Fans (n = 5,692)
Mid-Value Fans (n = 9,620)
High-Value Fans (n = 5,903)

5.4 **The percent who have received or are likely to receive the COVID-19 vaccine based on party affiliation.**
N = 23,918.
Q1: Have you received a vaccine to prevent COVID-19?
Q2: How likely are you to get the COVID-19 vaccine?
Q3: Who did you vote for in the 2020 Presidential Election?

Next, we began tracking attitudes regarding vaccines — another polarized topic — as they became available in early 2021. Looking at the Value segments, we again identified patterns that hinted at the power of fandom. First, we saw the expected differences around vaccine acceptance between Democrats and Republicans. Second, for Democrats, fandom did not significantly impact vaccine acceptance. Among Republicans, however, we saw a real break between Non-Fans and Fans: Respondents who follow sports were considerably more likely to get vaccinated. Third, for Republicans and Unaffiliated respondents, we saw a steady progression of vaccine acceptance. So, what we found in COVID vaccine attitudes mirrored what we had seen in COVID protocols.

When we saw that pattern, it was like discovering a door to a new hallway in our own home. Could fandom exert some gravitational pull on otherwise polarized positions? We ventured down the hallway to find out.

FANDOM AND TRUST

"Trust is an essential elixir for public life and neighborly relations, and when Americans think about trust these days, they worry," states the 2019 Pew Report *Trust and Distrust in America*. According to this study,

> Some see fading trust as a sign of cultural sickness and national decline. Some also tie it to what they perceive to be increased loneliness and excessive individualism. About half of Americans (49%) link the decline in interpersonal trust to a belief that people are not as reliable as they used to be. Many ascribe shrinking trust to a political culture they believe is broken and spawns suspicion, even cynicism, about the ability of others to distinguish fact from fiction.[25]

As we pondered the relationship between fandom and COVID attitudes, it seemed to us a natural next step to examine trust — of one another and of institutions — through a fan lens.

To do so, we implemented the trust survey questions used by the Pew Report. The results were consistent with our previous findings pertaining to fans and friendships, wellbeing, and loneliness: Higher-value fans were more likely than lower-value and non-fans to agree that most people can be trusted and try to help others, and that it's better for folks to be trusting rather than skeptical.

Fig. 5.5

We also looked at a series of statements that measure respondents' trust that others will "do the right thing." Figures 5.6 and 5.7 illustrate the proportion of respondents who have "a great deal of confidence" (the highest point on a four-point scale) in the American people to "respect the rights of people who are not like them" and "have civil conversations with people who have different views from theirs." Notably, baseline trust levels are alarmingly low, underscoring the depth of our polarization problem. Why would we risk stepping out of our socially sorted bubbles when we perceive "outsiders" as disrespectful and uncivil? Moreover, we see equally low confidence levels among Democrats and Republicans: Both sides perceive these statements in the same way. Finally, we see a significant jump — more than double — in confidence levels between Non-Fans and High-Value Fans. This last point reinforces a refrain common by now: The bigger the fan, the higher their confidence in others.

Fig. 5.6, 5.7

Does this confidence in individuals extend also to institutions? Using the same four-point scale, we asked respondents to rate their degree of confidence that an institution will "do the right thing for the American people." These "institutions" include scientists, the military, police, professors, religious leaders, and the news media. As you'll see, the pattern holds.

Fig. 5.8

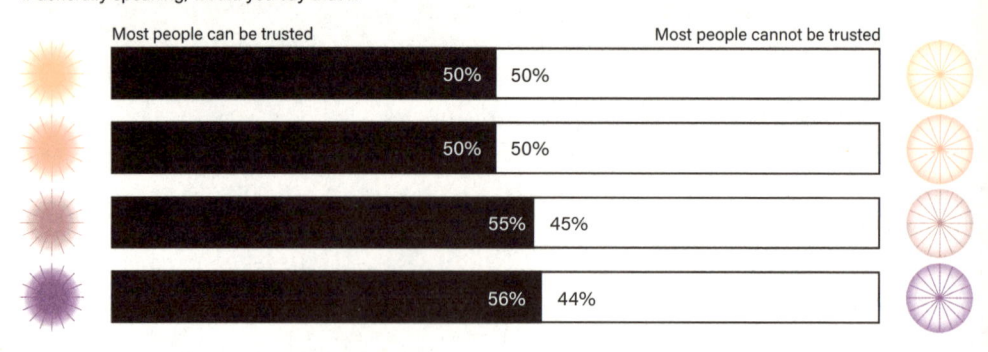

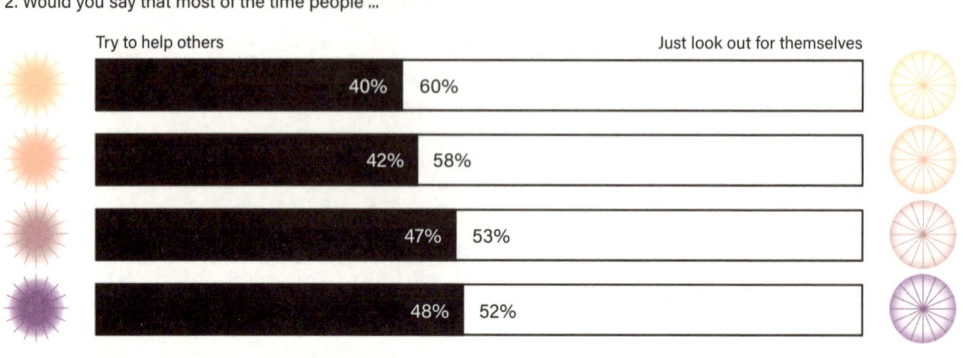

1. Generally speaking, would you say that ...

Most people can be trusted | Most people cannot be trusted

- Non-Fans: 50% / 50%
- Low-Value Fans: 50% / 50%
- Mid-Value Fans: 55% / 45%
- High-Value Fans: 56% / 44%

2. Would you say that most of the time people ...

Try to help others | Just look out for themselves

- Non-Fans: 40% / 60%
- Low-Value Fans: 42% / 58%
- Mid-Value Fans: 47% / 53%
- High-Value Fans: 48% / 52%

3. In most situations, do you think it's better for people to ...

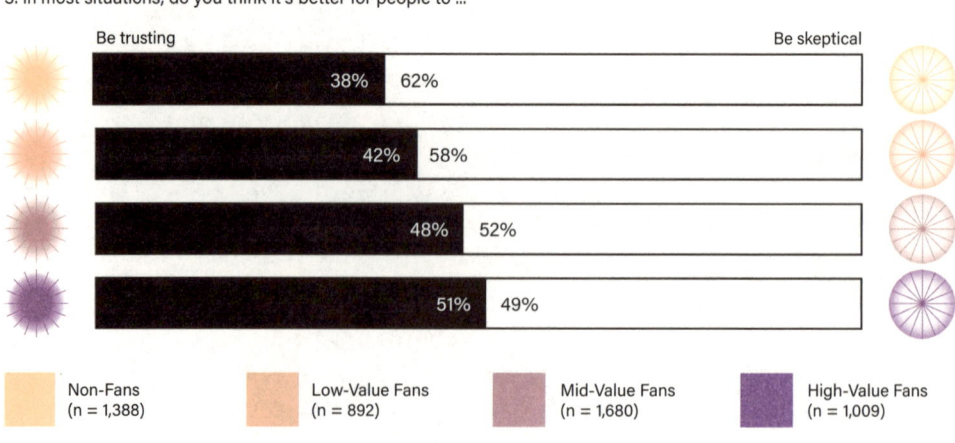

Be trusting | Be skeptical

- Non-Fans: 38% / 62%
- Low-Value Fans: 42% / 58%
- Mid-Value Fans: 48% / 52%
- High-Value Fans: 51% / 49%

Non-Fans (n = 1,388)
Low-Value Fans (n = 892)
Mid-Value Fans (n = 1,680)
High-Value Fans (n = 1,009)

5.5 **The percent who agree with trust statements.** N = 4,969.
Q1: Generally speaking, would you say that ... (topmost graph)
Q2: Would you say that most of the time people ... (middle graph)
Q3: In most situations, do you think it's better for people to ... (bottom graph)

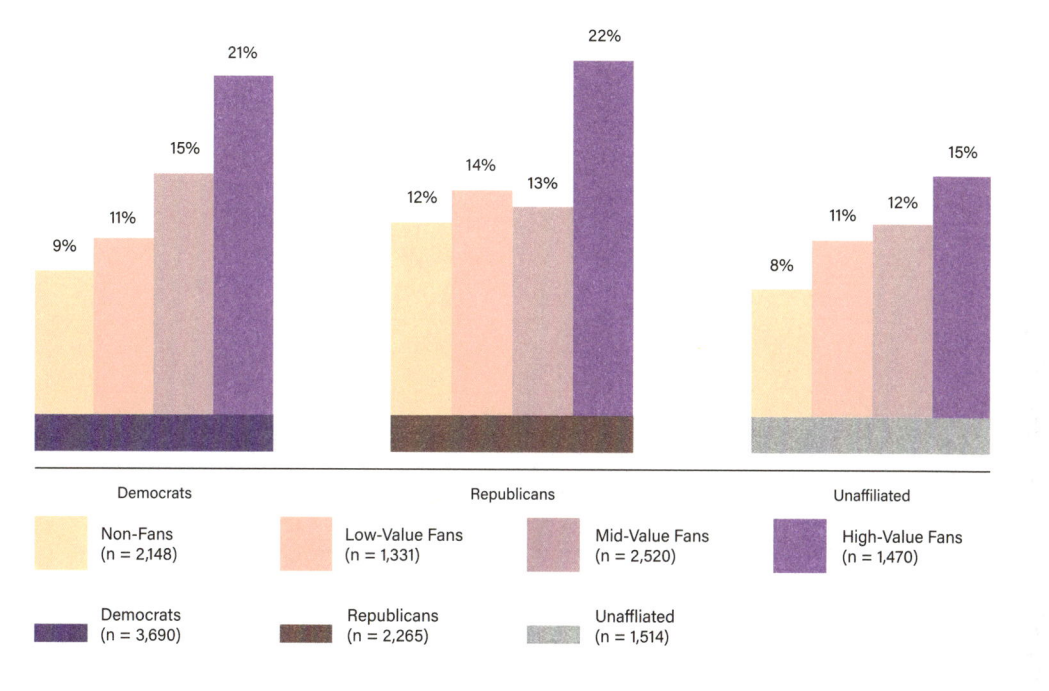

	Democrats	Republicans	Unaffiliated
Non-Fans	9%	12%	8%
Low-Value Fans	11%	14%	11%
Mid-Value Fans	15%	13%	12%
High-Value Fans	21%	22%	15%

Non-Fans (n = 2,148)
Low-Value Fans (n = 1,331)
Mid-Value Fans (n = 2,520)
High-Value Fans (n = 1,470)

Democrats (n = 3,690)
Republicans (n = 2,265)
Unaffiliated (n = 1,514)

5.6 **The percent who have a great deal of confidence in Americans to respect the rights of people who are not like them.** N = 7,469.
Q1: Generally speaking, how much confidence, if any, do you have in the American people to respect the rights of people who are not like them?
Q2: Who did you vote for in the 2020 Presidential Election?

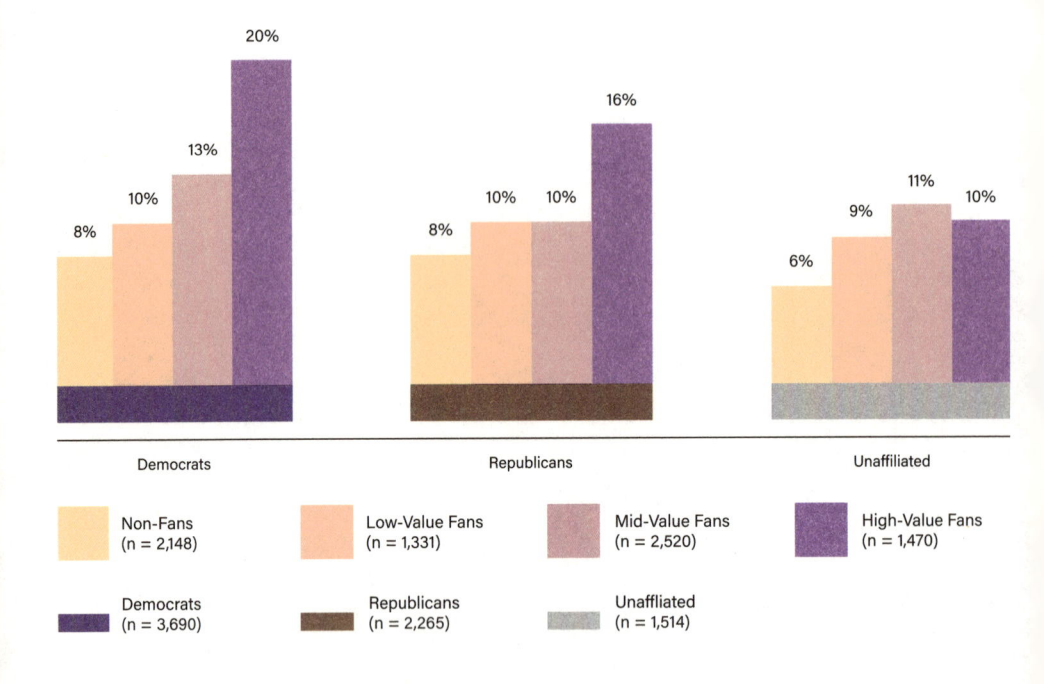

Democrats

- Non-Fans: 8%
- Low-Value Fans: 10%
- Mid-Value Fans: 13%
- High-Value Fans: 20%

Republicans

- Non-Fans: 8%
- Low-Value Fans: 10%
- Mid-Value Fans: 10%
- High-Value Fans: 16%

Unaffiliated

- Non-Fans: 6%
- Low-Value Fans: 9%
- Mid-Value Fans: 11%
- High-Value Fans: 10%

Legend:
- Non-Fans (n = 2,148)
- Low-Value Fans (n = 1,331)
- Mid-Value Fans (n = 2,520)
- High-Value Fans (n = 1,470)
- Democrats (n = 3,690)
- Republicans (n = 2,265)
- Unaffiliated (n = 1,514)

5.7 **The percent who have a great deal of confidence in Americans to have civil conversations with people with different views.** N = 7,469.
Q1: Generally speaking, how much confidence, if any, do you have in the American people to have civil conversations with people with different views?
Q2: Who did you vote for in the 2020 Presidential Election?

THE POLARIZATION PROBLEM

Scientists

- Non-Fans: 34%
- Low-Value Fans: 33%
- Mid-Value Fans: 39%
- High-Value Fans: 44%

Military

- Non-Fans: 29%
- Low-Value Fans: 33%
- Mid-Value Fans: 39%
- High-Value Fans: 41%

Police

- Non-Fans: 23%
- Low-Value Fans: 26%
- Mid-Value Fans: 30%
- High-Value Fans: 30%

Professors

- Non-Fans: 15%
- Low-Value Fans: 16%
- Mid-Value Fans: 22%
- High-Value Fans: 25%

Religious Leaders

- Non-Fans: 14%
- Low-Value Fans: 14%
- Mid-Value Fans: 18%
- High-Value Fans: 22%

News Media

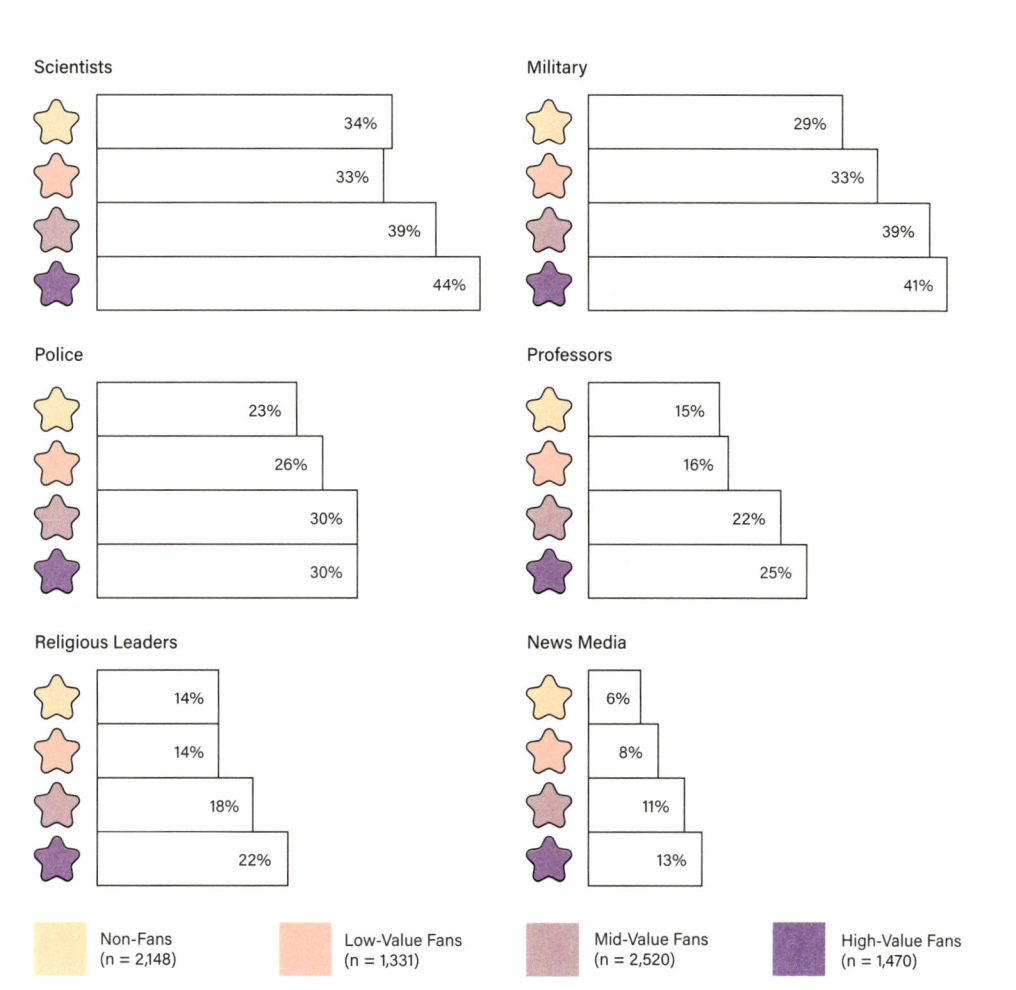

- Non-Fans: 6%
- Low-Value Fans: 8%
- Mid-Value Fans: 11%
- High-Value Fans: 13%

Non-Fans (n = 2,148)
Low-Value Fans (n = 1,331)
Mid-Value Fans (n = 2,520)
High-Value Fans (n = 1,470)

5.8   **The percent who have a great deal of confidence in specific institutions.** N = 7,469.
Q: Generally speaking, how much confidence, if any, do you have in the following institutions to do the right thing for the American people?

Fig. 5.9   We selected these institutions for a reason: Supporting or opposing these institutions has become a signal of in-group credentials. Generally, trust or mistrust in each one respectively aligns with the sorted mega-identities labeled "Democrat" and "Republican." Figure 5.9 highlights institutions associated with the "Democrat" identity: science, academia, and news media. As you see, confidence in them rises and falls along political divides. Yet, once again, within both political parties we see a rise in confidence levels along with a rise in fandom. It's worth nothing that confidence in the news media is low overall — and virtually nonexistent among Republicans — so we looked at the other end of the spectrum, focusing on those who have "no confidence" in the news media. There, we see among Republicans a decline in those with "no confidence" as we move from Non-Fans to High-Value Fans. So, even with an institution as maligned as the news media, we still see an increase in confidence levels among Republicans who are High-Value Fans.

Now, let's look at institutions more commonly associated with Republicans: the military, police, and religious leaders. Predictably, fewer Democrats reported "a great deal of confidence" in these institutions than Republicans. Interestingly, Democrats' trust in these institutions grows alongside their fandom.

What can we extrapolate from these results? A hope that, even within deeply entrenched political identities, people's attitudes can be influenced by fandom — and specifically, we contend, by the social connection that fandom creates. After all, unlike the mega-identities that sort us into separate enclaves of like-minded people, sports fandom crosses identity categories, allowing us to experience more social interaction with people from all walks of life, and to develop a greater sense of belonging, not only within our in-groups, but within the world at large. When we are closely connected to a robust social network, as highly engaged fans are, we are more likely to develop trust in others. Here we see the potential power of fandom's social impact: Regardless of political orientation, it appears, fandom can move seemingly intractable positions.

FANDOM AND SOCIAL JUSTICE

As we were investigating COVID and trust in relation to fandom, we were on a parallel path to understand attitudes toward the social justice demonstrations sparked by the murder of George Floyd on May 25, 2020. As the country was erupting into protest, live sports were slowly beginning to return from COVID postponements, and players and leagues began to outwardly support the social justice movement. With this story dominating the news cycle, we were keen to track sentiment among fans and non-fans alike. We began by asking about approval of the protest movement. Overall, as Figure 5.10 illustrates, the bigger the fan, the higher the approval.

Fig. 5.10

Of course, views on race diverge with political affiliation. When we looked at attitudes by political party, the divide was stark: Nearly a 60-point difference between Democrats and Republicans. Interestingly, however, approval of the protest movement rose steadily across Value segments within each political party. Again, the bigger the fan, the higher the approval, regardless of party affiliation.

Fig. 5.11

Attitudes regarding race are influenced by a variety of demographic factors, including education, age, and religious affiliation. Many of these same demographic factors also intersect with fandom. So, to ensure that these demographics were not influencing the shift we were seeing among fans, we looked at attitudes toward the social justice movement across these demographic variables. As you'll see in Figure 5.12, no matter the demographic cut, the bigger the fan, the higher the approval. Related, the lower the

Fig. 5.12

Scientists

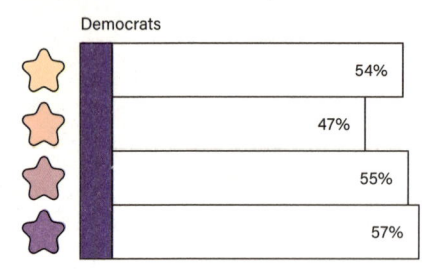

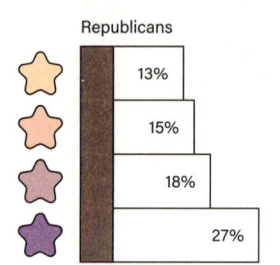

Democrats
- 54%
- 47%
- 55%
- 57%

Republicans
- 13%
- 15%
- 18%
- 27%

Professors

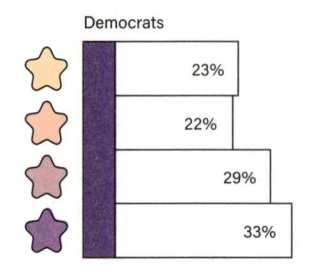

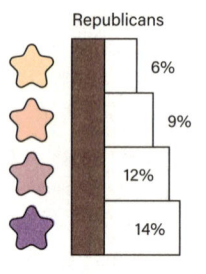

Democrats
- 23%
- 22%
- 29%
- 33%

Republicans
- 6%
- 9%
- 12%
- 14%

News Media

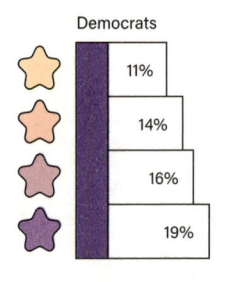

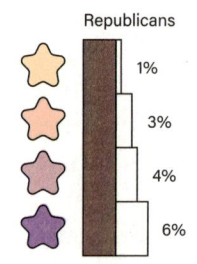

Democrats
- 11%
- 14%
- 16%
- 19%

Republicans
- 1%
- 3%
- 4%
- 6%

News Media, No Confidence

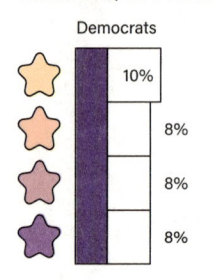

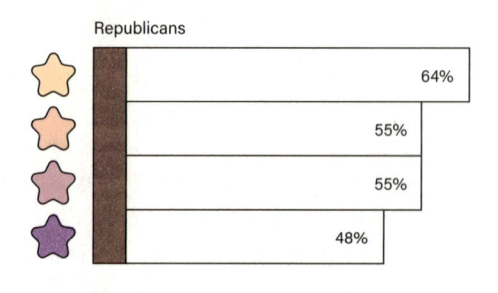

Democrats
- 10%
- 8%
- 8%
- 8%

Republicans
- 64%
- 55%
- 55%
- 48%

Military

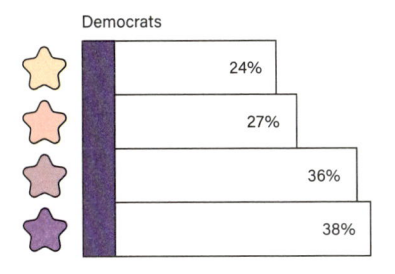

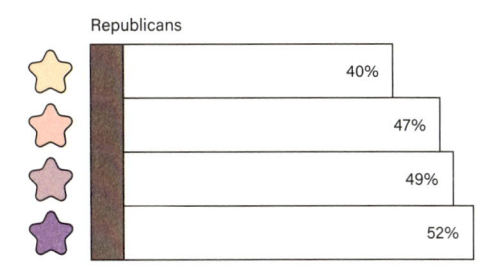

Democrats
- 24%
- 27%
- 36%
- 38%

Republicans
- 40%
- 47%
- 49%
- 52%

Police

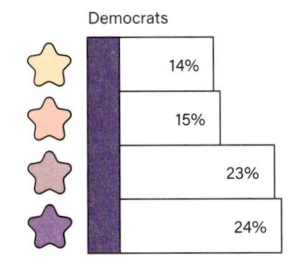

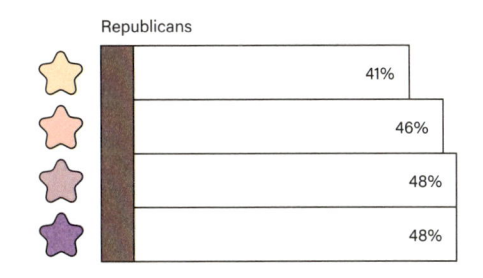

Democrats
- 14%
- 15%
- 23%
- 24%

Republicans
- 41%
- 46%
- 48%
- 48%

Religious Leaders

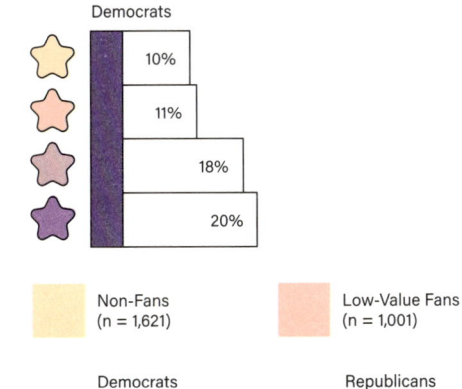

Democrats
- 10%
- 11%
- 18%
- 20%

Republicans
- 20%
- 21%
- 22%
- 27%

Non-Fans (n = 1,621)
Low-Value Fans (n = 1,001)
Mid-Value Fans (n = 2,064)
High-Value Fans (n = 1,269)

Democrats (n = 3,690)
Republicans (n = 2,265)

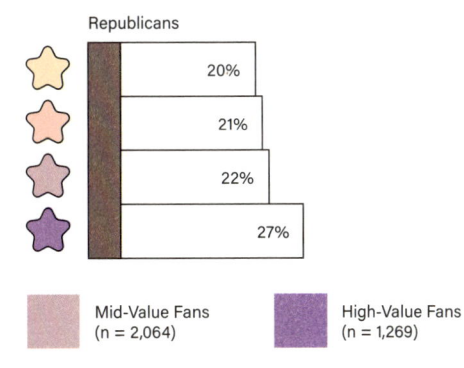

5.9 **The percent who have a great deal of confidence in specific institutions.** N = 5,955.
Q1: Generally speaking, how much confidence, if any, do you have in the following institutions to do the right thing for the Americn people?
Q2: Who did you vote for in the 2020 Presidential Election?

46% 44% 49% 57%

Non-Fans (n = 4,497)   Low-Value Fans (n = 7,957)   Mid-Value Fans (n = 13,660)   High-Value Fans (n = 8,196)

5.10 **The percent who approve of the social justice movement.** N = 34,130.
Q: In 2020, the killings of George Floyd in Minnesota, Ahmaud Arbery in Georgia, and Breonna Taylor in Kentucky, among others, sparked a protest movement with rallies occuring in all 50 states. How much do you approve of this protest movement?

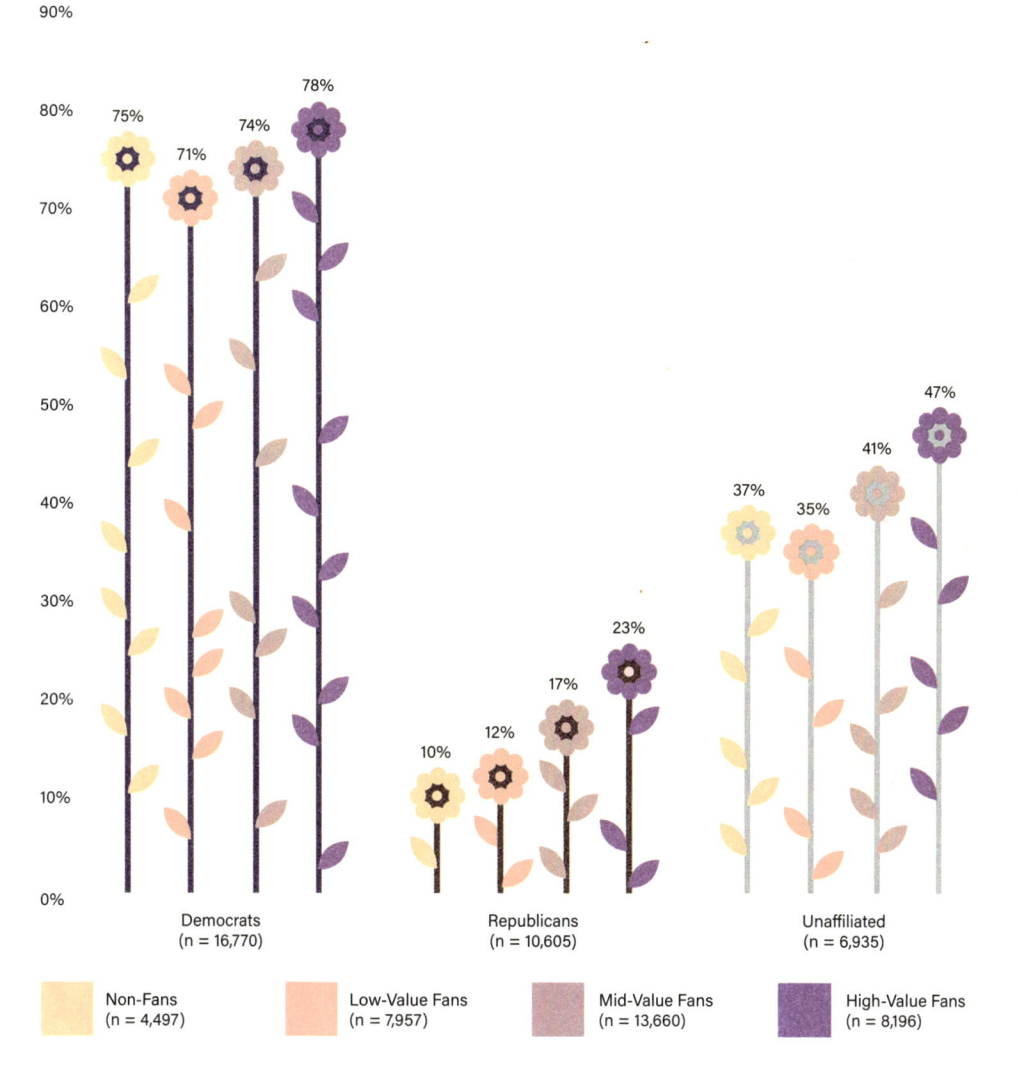

	%
Democrats (n = 16,770)	Non-Fans: 75%, Low-Value Fans: 71%, Mid-Value Fans: 74%, High-Value Fans: 78%
Republicans (n = 10,605)	Non-Fans: 10%, Low-Value Fans: 12%, Mid-Value Fans: 17%, High-Value Fans: 23%
Unaffiliated (n = 6,935)	Non-Fans: 37%, Low-Value Fans: 35%, Mid-Value Fans: 41%, High-Value Fans: 47%

Non-Fans (n = 4,497)
Low-Value Fans (n = 7,957)
Mid-Value Fans (n = 13,660)
High-Value Fans (n = 8,196)

5.11 **The percent who approve of the social justice movement based on party affiliation.** N = 34,130. Q: In 2020, the killings of George Floyd in Minnesota, Ahmaud Arbery in Georgia, and Breonna Taylor in Kentucky, among others, sparked a protest movement with rallies occuring in all 50 states. How much do you approve of this protest movement?

THE POLARIZATION PROBLEM

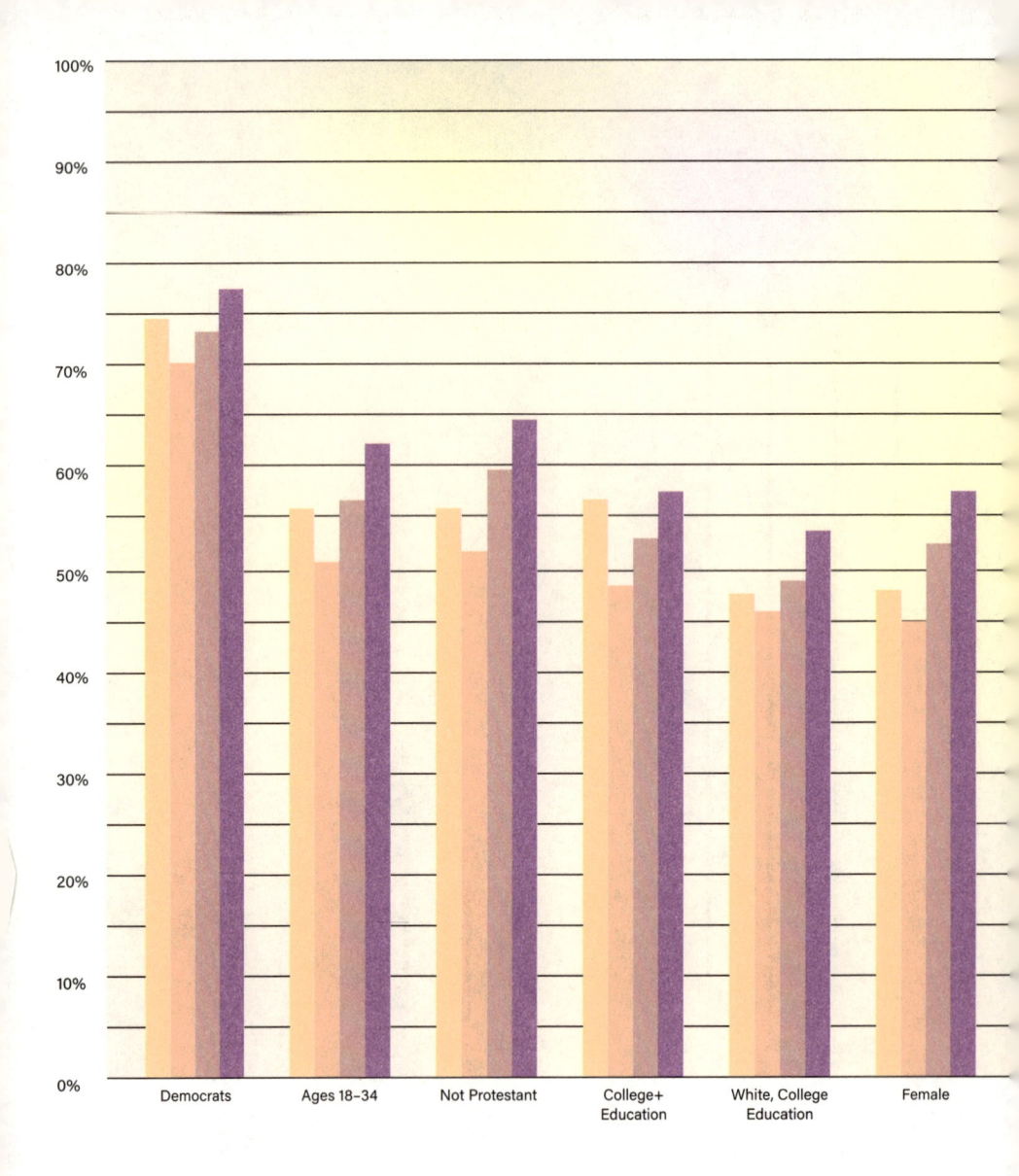

baseline starting point for a given demographic cut, the larger the overall growth in approval from Non-Fan to High-Value Fan.

The social justice movement results were so intriguing that we began to explore attitudes toward race from a different angle. We borrowed the following question from Pew: "According to the U.S. Census Bureau, in the next 25 to 30 years, African Americans, Latinos, and people of Asian descent will make up a majority of the population. In general, do you think that this is a good thing, bad thing, or neither good nor bad?" The results follow a familiar progression: The bigger the fan, the more likely to view growing diversity as a benefit for the country. Just like respondents' attitudes about the social justice movement, within each political group we see a lift in support for this idea across Value segments.

Fig. 5.13

Clearly, something big was happening here. During a highly contentious time in our nation's history, with a pandemic raging and protests erupting, social commentators were focused on the ever-widening, seemingly unbridgeable gap between factions. And, certainly, we see that gap illustrated in these charts. But our analysis also gives us reason for hope. We have observed a force — fandom — that seems to create positive shifts within those factions, bringing people closer together. Fans consistently demonstrate more considered attitudes toward the issues of the day, arguably more so than anyone would have imagined or given them credit for.

To recap: the bigger the fan, the more likely to follow COVID protocols, the more trusting the outlook on individuals and institutions, and the more open the views on social justice. But why? Before we answer that question, we want to introduce you to Sean Oliver.

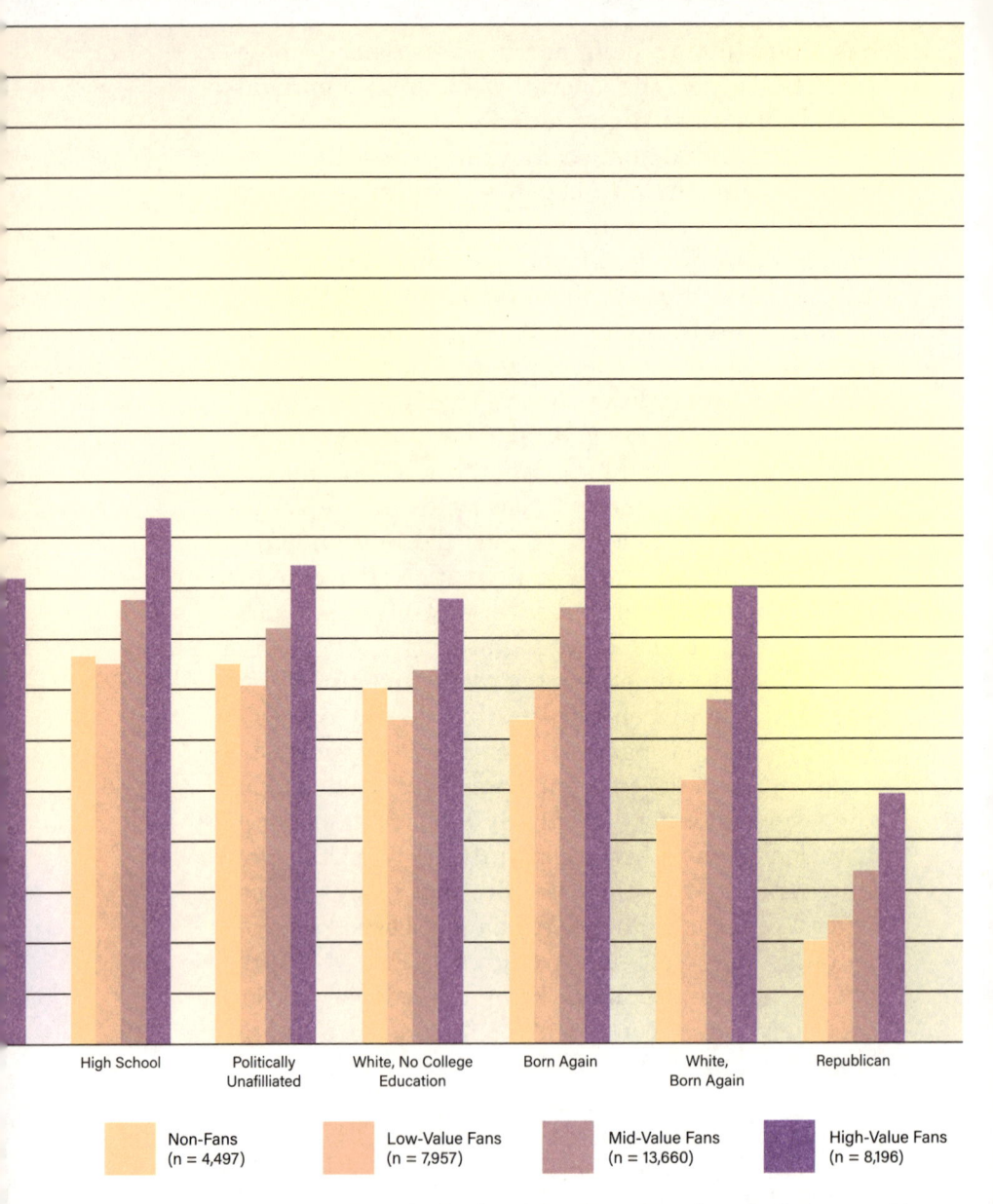

| | Non-Fans (n = 4,497) | | Low-Value Fans (n = 7,957) | | Mid-Value Fans (n = 13,660) | | High-Value Fans (n = 8,196) |

5.12 **The percent approving of the social justice movement based on specific demographic groups.** N = 34,130
Q1: In 2020, the killings of George Floyd in Minnesota, Ahmaud Arbery in Georgia, and Breonna Taylor in Kentucky, among others, sparked a protest movement with rallies occuring in all 50 states. How much do you approve of this protest movement?
Q2: Who did you vote for in the 2020 Presidential Election?

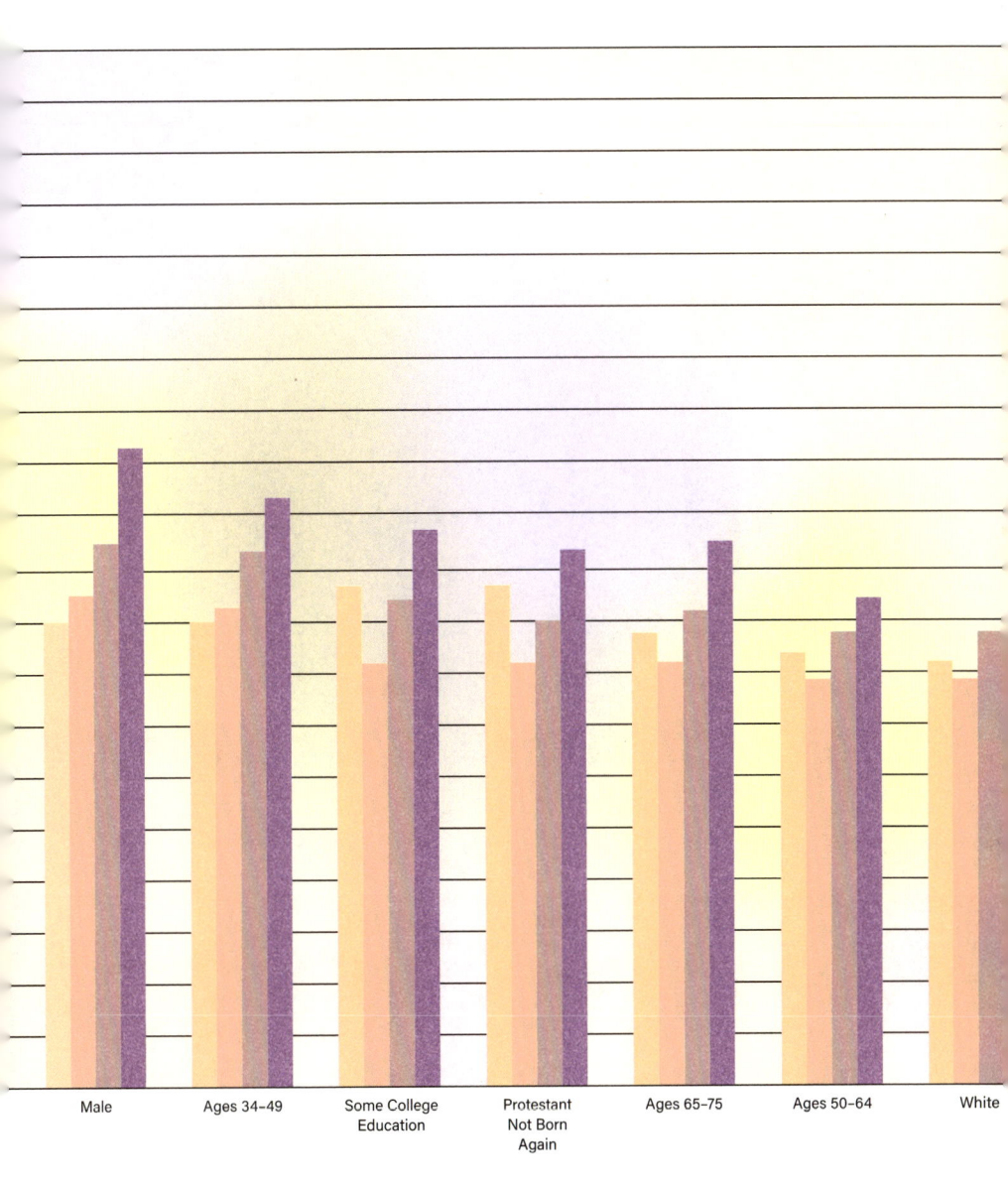

Male   Ages 34–49   Some College Education   Protestant Not Born Again   Ages 65–75   Ages 50–64   White

153

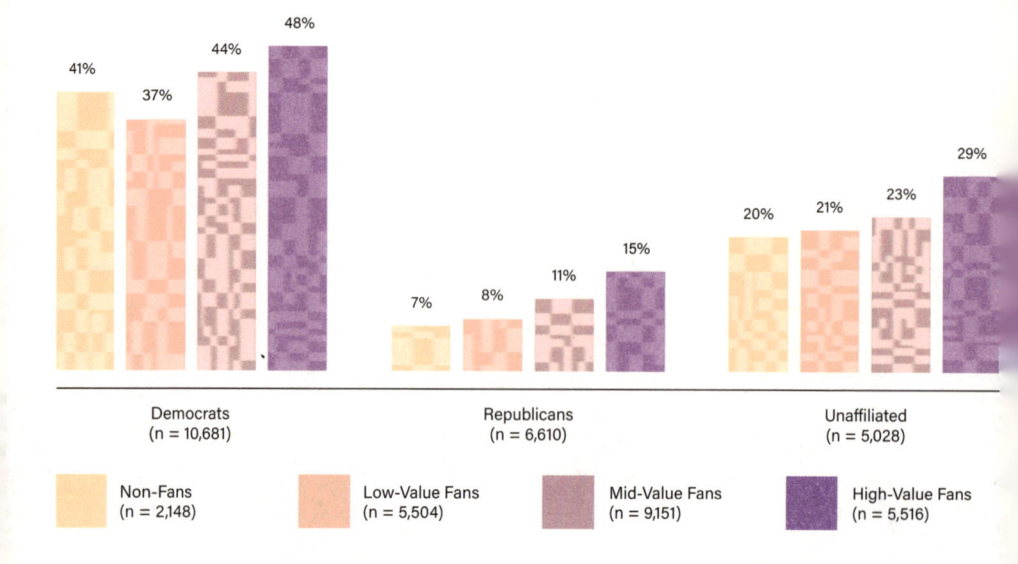

Chart data:

Democrats (n = 10,681): Non-Fans 41%, Low-Value Fans 37%, Mid-Value Fans 44%, High-Value Fans 48%

Republicans (n = 6,610): Non-Fans 7%, Low-Value Fans 8%, Mid-Value Fans 11%, High-Value Fans 15%

Unaffiliated (n = 5,028): Non-Fans 20%, Low-Value Fans 21%, Mid-Value Fans 23%, High-Value Fans 29%

Legend:
- Non-Fans (n = 2,148)
- Low-Value Fans (n = 5,504)
- Mid-Value Fans (n = 9,151)
- High-Value Fans (n = 5,516)

5.13 **The percent that view the country becoming majority minority as good for the country.** N = 22,319.
Q1: According to the U.S. Census Bureau, in the next 25 to 30 years, African Americans, Latinos, and people of Asian descent will make up a majority of the population. In general do you think that this is good for the country?
Q2: Who did you vote for in the 2020 Presidential Election?

SEAN'S STORY

When you regularly run focus groups, like we do, you occasionally run into a group participant who stands out as openly curious and courageously introspective. That's the person you call up after the group session to ask for some one-on-one time. In a focus group we conducted with viewers of daytime sports talk shows, that group participant was Sean Oliver.

Before his tenth birthday, Sean had already traveled more than most adults. "My dad did a lot of documentary filmmaking when I was a child," he told us. "So, I traveled a lot: six continents a couple times over by the time I was seven or eight." When Sean wasn't traveling, his childhood home bases were the Dominican Republic and Harlem, New York. That was until he landed in Los Angeles, feeling like a fish out of water. "By the time I was nine," he recalled to us, "I was six feet tall, and my English was okay, but because I had been traveling through Latin America so much, I was not really well versed on American culture." He got a "crash course on what it feels like to be Black in America," when his parents enrolled him in a private school that was predominantly white.

Predictably, because of his size, Sean was immediately recruited to play football and basketball. Alongside his athletic skills, he had also developed a deep knowledge of sports trivia, so much so that his father's friends called him "The Almanac." By the time we met him, Sean was a sought-after personal trainer, a sponsored bodybuilder, and the founder of a film production company. Also: Sean was still an almanac. As we would learn when we sat down with him in 2018 at his apartment in Reseda, California, Sean watched daytime sports talk shows to sharpen his take on the sports headlines of the day.

"You never know when someone might start a conversation about sports," he told us. "I want to be ready for that."

We asked for an example of this kind of encounter. "What do you know about Simi Valley?" Sean asked us. Then he proceeded to tell us a story that would change forever our conception of the potential power of fandom.

Just a couple days before our meeting, Sean had been out in Simi Valley, a historically conservative suburb of Los Angeles made famous as the site of the 1992 trial of four police officers indicted for brutalizing Black motorist Rodney King. There, Sean was visiting a woman he was dating, who happened to be white. After a workout at a local gym, the pair ducked into an iconic diner, The Egg House, for breakfast. As soon as they passed through the door, a couple of gray-haired white men sitting in a booth, clearly regulars, looked up from their newspapers in unison, took in the sight of Sean and his companion, then looked back at each other. Suddenly, Sean became acutely aware that he was the only Black person in the room. He braced himself for the worst, then heard one of the men say to the other, "Now, he's gotta play football." The second guy looked at Sean and asked, "Who do you play for?"

That question unspooled a conversation that continued, to his date's surprise, for the duration of their meal: a true exchange of ideas, questions, opinions, memories, and laughter. The banter was so jovial and familiar that Sean's date asked him, "Do you know these guys? Why do you keep talking to them?"

As Sean recounted this story for us, his demeanor shifted. He went from pleasantly reflective to — there's no other word for it — elated. He was smiling, chuckling, telling the story with his whole body. We called his attention to that: "You had fun talking to those guys."

"Yeah," he laughed, "I did. My personality comes out best when I'm talking about sports. It combines all my loves into one."

It first occurred to Sean that sports can create social connections when he was the new kid in town, playing on his middle-school basketball team. "If I got an A on a test, no one said, 'Hey, I want you to come to dinner because you got an A on the test.' But if I hit the winning shot, then they were like, 'Hey, come to my house.'" These days, Sean says, it's fandom more so than athleticism that enables him to connect. Sure, a stranger might start a conversation based on Sean's physique. But, he explained, "When they see that I'm an actual fan, we're going to have a stronger connection. We can break down every single team and every single athlete on that team. Now it's a conversation, now we have more of a friendship."

Something else, something potentially much bigger, is happening here, though. Sean knowingly uses those conversations to bridge social divisions. "I always feel like I have to be like an ambassador," he explained to us. "I have to showcase that I am not someone's fear; I am better than their fear." That's an unjust burden to have to shoulder, but Sean values the transformative experience: "You get to see someone's preconceived notions change. You can almost feel it. They're like, 'Wow, you're not that scary Black man the news always talks about. You care about pretty much the same stuff that I care about.'" Though he regularly finds himself shaking his head, thinking, "I can't believe people still think that way," he also finds hope in the process of dissolving stereotypes and building connections.

During our initial interview with Sean, in 2018, that's where his story ended. When we met up with him again, in 2021, he had gained some new insights on his Simi Valley experience.

This time, when he revisited The Egg House incident, he recalled the emotional weight of venturing into Simi Valley. Even well-traveled Sean, with his extraordinarily optimistic temperament, felt wary of venturing out of his geographic bubble. "Everybody from LA was telling me, 'Be careful when you go out there. They hate Black people.'" In hindsight, he could see that he was "more on the defense. I had to create a shell. I was afraid someone was going to attack me because I was dating out of my race."

Sean carried that fear when he went to the grocery store with his girlfriend. Working out at the gym with her, he felt that edge. When he showed up in the doorway of The Egg House that morning in 2018, and those two white men looked up at him, he expected the worst from them. "I was thinking they were going to come at me, and then they were talking about sports, and I realized, 'Oh, they don't hate me,' and then, 'Not only do they not hate me, but they enjoy my company, and I'm actually comfortable.'" No wonder Sean was so elated by the conversation: In a matter of minutes, it dismantled his fear and replaced it with joyful engagement in his favorite pastime.

"I didn't realize it until right now," Sean told us in 2021, "but that was a crossroads moment for me."

What had changed? Sean paused for a moment to reflect. Then a new insight emerged: For all the years he'd served as a self-appointed "ambassador," he had thought of himself as changing other people's preconceived notions about him. But now he understood that he, too, carried preconceived notions about others. When those guys at The Egg House engaged Sean in conversation, they quickly morphed from potential threat into fellow fans excited to meet another person who shared in their passion. "This sports stuff actually made a difference in all our lives," Sean mused.

Make no mistake: Sean's not saying that sports fandom is an antidote to racism. But he is advocating for the power of fandom to build bridges across social lines. Maybe those guys were looking for a chance to dispel Sean's preconceived notions about them, too. Fandom gave them the opportunity.

COMMON GROUND

What does Sean's story teach us about connecting across polarized groups? At least in part, it shows us that the process begins with contact.

American psychologist Gordon Allport published his now-classic text, *The Nature of Prejudice*, in 1979.[26] In it, he concludes that prejudice and conflict between groups diminish their interactions with each other under favorable conditions. This idea makes intuitive sense: More contact with more people naturally broadens one's perspective. Though it seems obvious to us today, Allport's hypothesis was debated for decades. Finally, in 2006, after years of academic discussion regarding the viability of Contact Theory, psychologists Thomas Pettigrew and Linda Tropp reviewed more than 500 previous studies with approximately 250,000 research participants. Their conclusion: the available data supported Allport's hypothesis.[27] As it turns out, contact matters.

Why does something as simple as contact produce such transformative results? For a few reasons. First, in-groups often carry assumptions about out-groups, especially those with whom they have few interactions. When they do meet, the contact is an opportunity to replace those assumptions with reality, which relieves anxiety and helps dispel prejudice. Second, contact increases empathy, helping people, in Pettigrew and Tropp's words, "sense how out-group members feel and view the world." Third, as psychologist John Dovidio suggests, positive intergroup interactions can prompt "recategorization," which "changes the conceptual representations of the different groups from an 'us versus them' orientation to a more inclusive 'we.'"[28]

There's no shortage of scholarship affirming the importance of cross-group contact. In short, as author Brené Brown has famously said, "It's hard to hate people up close."[29]

Therein lies the power of sports. Fandom initiates contact between people of all stripes, and that cross-group contact has a positive impact on a fan's worldview.

Why did fans take COVID protocols more seriously? Why are fans more confident in their fellow human beings? Why does support for social justice and diversity grow along the Value Scale? Because highly engaged sports fans have regular contact with people outside their in-groups. Better yet, they share a passion and an identity — sports fan — with a population diverse in ideology, race, religion, and every other social category. When people meet in the depolarized territory of fandom, it might sound like they're just talking sports, but underneath that language, something much more profound is happening. Even a fleeting interaction can lift the veil of our assumptions about one another, allowing us to recognize our shared humanity, to shift our perspectives, and to build trust, confidence, and empathy. Fans recognize that fandom builds bridges, and they use that ability, at scale. Even across wide social divisions, no matter which side we stand on, we sports fans have something we can talk about, together.

06 Fandom as Identity

So: the bigger the sports fan, the more friends. The more friends, the more social interaction. And the more social interaction, the more contact with a wider variety of people. As we saw in Sean Oliver's story, that contact can change how you see the world. For all these reasons, Contact Theory offers one explanation for the positive patterns we see in sports fans' attitudes toward issues and institutions — attitudes that can run counter to hardened political identities. Contact, in and of itself, is a good thing, a powerful thing. But it's not the whole story. There's something deeper going on in sports fandom that speaks to the power of identity.

In the previous chapter, we introduced the idea of "mega-identities." For example, identifying as "Democrat" or "Republican" can signal a whole host of identities that have nothing to do with policy positions. Identities or positions like "non-white," "urban," and "non-religious" signal Democrat, for example, while "white," "rural," and "evangelical" signal Republican. The alignment of these different identities under a single mega-identity is, arguably, the core problem leading to our polarized situation. Recall Lillianna Mason's indelible words: "This is the American identity crisis. Not that we have partisan identities, we've always had those. The crisis emerges when partisan identities fall into alignment with other social identities, stoking our intolerance of each other to levels that are unsupported by our degrees of political disagreement."

How can we mitigate the negative side effects of these highly aligned, overlapping identity categories? Mason argues that it's possible to "dampen" those effects by cutting across them. The effects of partisanship and bias on action can be mitigated, she explains, when a person is a member of one party and also a member of a social group generally associated with the opposing party. The opposite is also true:

When a member of one party also socializes with a group of people "mostly made up of fellow partisans, the biasing and polarizing effect of partisanship can grow stronger."

The operative word here is "dampen." Mason, of course, isn't suggesting cross-cutting identities are a cure-all for our polarization problem. She's pointing to the root cause of polarization and identifying a phenomenon — cross-cutting identities — that can reduce, by degrees, some of its toxic side-effects.

To demonstrate, she looks at the impact that cross-cutting identities have on one's disdain for the other political side. Using data from the American National Election Survey — an opinion survey that has tracked political attitudes for decades — she analyzed responses to a "feeling thermometer." This sort of questionnaire asks respondents to rate their feeling toward a political party on a zero to 100 scale, where zero is "cold" and 100 is "hot." She found that strong partisans with more cross-cutting identities had "warmer" feelings for the other side than more moderate partisans with more aligned identities. It's not ideology that's driving disdain for the other side, it's our increasingly aligned identities. In other words, polarization is not a policy problem; it's an identity problem.

The psychological phenomenon of "Social Identity Complexity" helps us understand this dampening effect. The term was coined by social psychologists Marilyn Brewer and Sonia Roccas, who examined the psychological effects of holding multiple identities.[30] It breaks down like this: We all carry multiple social identities, including, for example, gender, race, religion, family roles, profession, geographic location, and more. The more our identities align, the simpler our makeup; the less they align, the more complex our makeup. We all exist somewhere along this continuum from simple to complex.

Sometimes our identities align neatly, one overlapping with the other. Think about a white, Republican, evangelical Christian who lives in Colby, Kansas (pop. 5,000), in what is thought to be the most politically conservative county, in a solidly Red state. White, evangelical, rural, and Republican are all distinct in-groups, and they have a high degree of overlap. That is, so many people hold simultaneous membership in all these groups that it's easy to think of members of these different groups as members of one, unified group. Brewer and Roccas call this a "simple" social identity. "A simple social identity is likely to be accompanied by the perception that any individual who is an out-group member on one dimension is also an out-group member on all others."

Now, let's play with this "degree of complexity" idea. Imagine a different person: a white, evangelical Republican, who resides in Queens, New York. This person's social identities include "urban," which overlaps less with white, evangelical, and Republican. As a result, this person's social identity gains a degree of complexity. This works in any direction: a non-white, non-religious Democrat from a rural area has a more complex social identity than a non-white, non-religious Democrat from an urban area.

Why does all this matter? Because research shows that identity complexity reduces bias. When someone in your in-group is also simultaneously a member of an out-group, the bias you have toward that out-group is reduced. Brewer and Roccas take this idea a step further and contend that complex social identities don't just impact feelings of bias toward specific out-groups, but actually change bias toward out-groups in general. In other words, complex social identities can change how we view the world beyond our specific in- and out-groups.

There are a few distinct reasons for this. The first has to do with how we define those groups. When you have a complex identity, the distinctions between groups become less salient. Think about a binary: If X is the opposite of Y, then you can define X simply by being "not Y." In this case the distinctions between X and Y matter a lot, because features of X and Y become acutely definitional. Adding degrees of complexity, as Brewer and Roccas explain, "make[s] social categorization more complex and reduce[s] the magnitude of in-group/out-group distinctions."

The second reason why complexity reduces bias pertains to self-definition. We all use our set of social identities to establish our sense of self. The more complex one's social identity, the less pull any one of those identities will have. Imagine two monuments. One of the monuments rests on three columns, while the other rests on nine. If one of the three columns starts to crumble, then the first monument is likely to fall. But if one of the nine columns starts to crumble, there's a good chance that that monument survives because it has so many others to fall back on. Similarly, if a person's self-concept is built on a few, highly aligned identities, that person will be more susceptible to perceiving a threat to any one of these identities as a direct threat to their sense of self. On the flip side, as Roccas and Brewers state, "multiple group memberships reduce the importance of any one social identity for satisfying an individual's need for belonging and self-definition." So, if a person's self-concept is built out of multiple, unaligned identities, that person is less likely to perceive a threat to one of these identities as a threat to their very being. Complexity dilutes the salience of any single identity.

Finally, people with complex social identities generally need to think and work harder to recognize and interpret information about their various in-groups, and to develop strategies for navigating membership in a variety of groups that, at least on the surface, don't seem to have much to do with one another. In other words, they are constantly flexing what might be thought of as their "identity awareness muscle." The more you flex this kind of thinking, the stronger it gets, increasing your comfort with ambiguity, uncertainty, and the very concept of identity — all of which tend to coincide with "tolerance-related values."

Okay, so that's the Cliffs Notes version of Social Identity Complexity and its impact on bias. But how does this relate to sports fandom? Well, our contention is that sports fandom — particularly in connection to a team — can operate as an identity category strong enough to influence a fan's overall social outlook. This idea alone adds depth to our understanding of fandom as a driver of more accepting, trusting, community-minded attitudes. What's more, the "team fan" identity has the potential to cross-cut a diverse array of other identities. In other words, there are white Dallas Cowboy fans and Black Dallas Cowboy fans, rural Dallas Cowboy fans and urban Dallas Cowboy fans, Republican Dallas Cowboy fans and Democrat Dallas Cowboy fans. As a result, adding this identity — Dallas Cowboy fan — to a sports fan's identity inherently adds complexity.

You might be thinking, "There's no way my Dallas Cowboys fandom is equivalent to my identity as a Catholic or a Jew or a New Yorker or Southerner." We, too, were initially hesitant to equate team fandom to more traditional identities. But then we considered just how common it is for people to fly a team flag outside their home (or use a team logo as an avatar on social media), to stick their team's logo on their bumpers (or tattoo it on their arms), to name their dogs (or their kids) after their favorite players. The reality is that, for fans, fandom is a fundamental component of their identity. Qualitatively, we've asked this question of sports fans in countless interviews: How important is your fandom relative to other identities?

For the engaged, High-Value fan, the answer is immediate and intuitive: Fandom is a fundamental component of their identity. They are just as quick to introduce themselves as, say, a Broncos fan as they are a biker or a Buddhist or a banker.

We have explored this idea quantitatively, too, asking respondents to rank a set of identities in order of personal importance and testing how team fandom ranks relative to other common identities like race, religion, and nationality. Again, higher-value fans were more likely to rank their sports team identity in the top three (of eight) identities. In fact, 42% of High-Value Fans rank their sports team in their top three. For these people, identity categories like race, religion, or nationality can carry relatively less importance than their fan identities.

Fig. 6.1

A highly ranked fan identity creates a set of conditions that can activate Social Identity Complexity, generating those "tolerance-related values." How? We can think of no better way to answer that question than to introduce you to Dallas Cowboy fan Stephen Chukumba.

THE COWBOY CONNECTION

Stephen Chukumba is the second of five children born to Nigerian parents who immigrated to the United States. Diplomatic work initially brought the family to the US, but when civil war broke out in their home country, the Chukumbas — as members of a persecuted ethnic group — could not return. Catholic Charities, an organization that helps immigrants and refugees settle in the US, took them in, and the Chukumba family grew roots in new soil.

As a Black boy, a Nigerian, a US citizen, and a child of immigrants, Stephen already had a complex social identity. And then his mom, Bridgit, unwittingly added another important identity to the mix: Dallas Cowboys fan. To differentiate between her

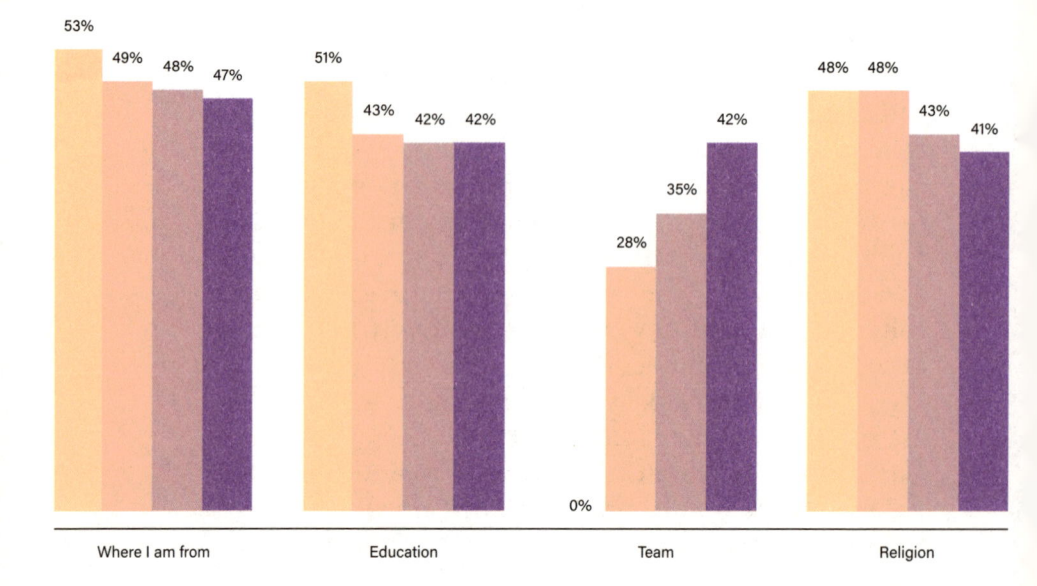

	Where I am from	Education	Team	Religion
	53%	51%	0%	48%
	49%	43%	28%	48%
	48%	42%	35%	43%
	47%	42%	42%	41%

FANDOM AS IDENTITY

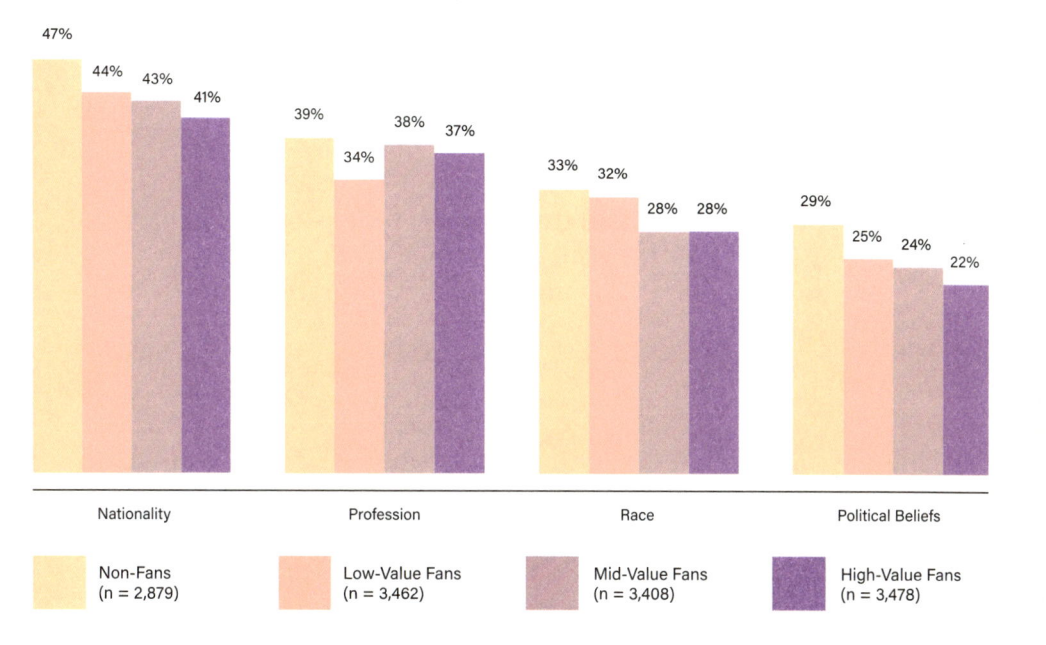

	Nationality	Profession	Race	Political Beliefs
Non-Fans (n = 2,879)	47%	39%	33%	29%
Low-Value Fans (n = 3,462)	44%	34%	32%	25%
Mid-Value Fans (n = 3,408)	43%	38%	28%	24%
High-Value Fans (n = 3,478)	41%	37%	28%	22%

6.1 **The percent that rank identity in top three of eight.** N = 13,227.
Q: How would you rank these identities? Please rank from most important "1" to least important "8".

three young sons' belongings, she randomly assigned each child an NFL team. "I was the Cowboys," Stephen told us. "She got me Cowboy sheets, Cowboy PJs, Cowboy lunch boxes, Cowboy clothes. My brother Anthony got all things Philadelphia Eagles, so for him everything was green and white. My youngest brother got the Washington Redskins [Commanders]. My parents were from Nigeria, so this meant nothing to them outside of being able to coordinate their young boys' stuff."

Though they became fans "by default, not design," for the Chukumba brothers, these team associations influenced the courses of their lives. "I'm fifty-one, my brother's fifty, my other brother's forty-nine," says Stephen. "All our lives we've been this way about these teams."

For the first two decades of his fandom, luck was with Stephen in his random assignment to the Cowboys, who are known as "America's Team." "I was very happy being a Cowboys fan. I was like, 'We're America's Team, we've got more trophies and championships than you jokers.' I talked so much trash, so much mess," Stephen told us, shaking his head. "Around the time I was in law school, I realized that the shine of the Cowboys was starting to wane. They built this big stadium, but they would lose every home game in that stadium. It became embarrassing." He has toned down the trash talk, but his loyalty remains. "In my heart of hearts, I'm a Cowboys fan, and one day we're going to rise to the top. We're going to be champions again. And I've been saying that for the past fifteen, twenty years."

Despite the obvious frustrations, Stephen remains good-natured about it all — as boisterous in his despair as he once was in his triumph. "What I'm suffering today," he joked, "is the karma of my past ego, my past bravado. But I love my team. I will always love my team."

Since his childhood, Stephen has added many identities: New Jersey resident, Rutgers alum, Seton Hall alum, lawyer, father. When we asked him if he considers his "Cowboys Fan" identity to be as important as the rest, he didn't blink an eye: "It's as valid as every other form of identification." He continued: "You can say, 'I am Albanian' and other Albanians will automatically gravitate to you because there's a shared culture between you and this other person. Even if you're from the different ethnic groups, you're from Albania. It's the same thing with your sports team. I am part of the tribe of Dallas Cowboys, and now and forever will be a member of that tribe. I have things in common with those people. I have a shared suffering, a decades-long suffering. Only another Cowboy fan can truly appreciate how close we get to grabbing that brass ring and how it just gets snatched away from us every time."

We've heard this story before, from Nick Camfield, the Cubs fan we met in our introduction, and Greg Armstrong, the Knicks fan we met in Chapter 2: how a shared history, even a history of loss, binds the fan family together and, in Stephen's words, "creates a sense of intimacy, even among strangers." When he sees people in Cowboy regalia, he thinks, "That's my tribe." They can strike up a conversation as if they've been lifelong friends. "How do I have a random conversation with people I've never met before that is so intimate, so personal, so significant, that allows us to have that kind of connection, that allows us to feel good about having run into one another, even if it's just in passing? How does that happen in the absence of some fabric tying us together? I think that speaks to identity. Only members of the same community, who have that same mindset, can participate in that. It is like race, it is like ethnicity, it is like religion, it is like all these other markers, all these other identifiers, all the ways people classify themselves. It's like when Brothers pass each other on the street and give the nod. That nod says everything in just a slight inflection of the head. It tells me we're down with one another. It's the same thing with the fan identity. I strongly believe that."

What Stephen says about fan identity aligns with our contention that fandom operates as an identity on the level of things like race, religion, and nationality. Stephen's experience of fandom also serves as a perfect illustration of Social Identity Complexity in action. When we suggested to him that a complex social identity has the potential to reduce bias and discrimination against out-groups — and that adding team fandom to the mix can produce the necessary complexity — he just nodded along, as if he had already read Brewer and Roccas. Better, he lives the theory every day. Without prompting, he offered us a perfect description of fandom as a cross-cutting identity: "Yes, we're all Cowboys fans, so that's our identity, but within that, let's call it a silo, there are hundreds of different types. There's your Sikh, your Jews, your Muslim, your agnostic. There is your alt-right and your BLM. All kinds of people are collectively agreeing that we are in this family called the Cowboys, and because that supersedes everything that would otherwise divide us, we all can formulate thoughts that are not as homogeneous as the centers out of which we come." Exactly.

Importantly, when we recognize identity complexity in ourselves, we become more attuned to such complexity in others, which helps us develop the aforementioned "identity awareness muscle." To meet Stephen, an outspoken, quick-witted Black man sporting a mohawk, tattoos, and thick-rimmed Ray Bans, you might not immediately think "son of Nigerian immigrants." Because he is aware that this part of his story might be invisible to a stranger on the subway, he is also aware that the stranger on the subway could hold membership in identity groups he cannot see. As such, Stephen, and all people with complex social identities, moves through the world differently, with more openness and curiosity about the people he encounters.

"Too often we reduce people to the most common denominator, and then we make judgments based on that, but when you have all these layers of complexity," Stephen explained, you become "less reductionist in your own thinking because you recognize that things are not always what they seem. People who, presumably, are one thing, can in fact have layers of complexity underneath." In this way, identity complexity lends to a greater capacity for critical thinking, for dealing with ambiguities. As a result, "I have a much greater capacity to think diverse thoughts, to appreciate divergent arguments, to accept non-traditional lines of thinking or concepts, because I myself am a complex creature."

As the distinctions between in- and out-groups become less salient, as that identity-awareness muscle strengthens, fandom becomes a training ground for communicating across differences. As Stephen put it, "In this space, we can have broader concepts. We can disagree over whether Zeke should be playing or not, and that conversation is just about Zeke and his last ten carries versus Pollard. We can now have all these conversations that have nothing to do with what we believe religiously, politically, or otherwise. But we're capable of having a conversation where we can differ about something that we both care about. Then you can extend it to having conversations about other things that are not related to football in a way that is respectful, that allows us to have a dialogue, that allows me to actually hear your point and not just discount you because you come out of this other bag that I don't agree with, because I come out of this other bag that says your way of thinking is wrong." At the end of the day, in Stephen's words, "The fact that there's diversity within our families enables us to be less myopic and hidebound than we would be were we not fans of sports."

The power of the fan identity stretches far beyond creating a sense of belonging amongst strangers. Ultimately, fandom is a place where Contact Theory and Social Identity Complexity intersect. As a cross-cutting identity, "Cowboys fan" brings together members of different in-groups in both the shared space of a football stadium, and the shared identity of "Cowboys fan." That's where the magic happens: Contact with fellow fans gives us the opportunity to connect with perceived "others" over a common interest, and thereby to dissolve preconceived notions about each other.

But adding complexity to our identities through fandom doesn't simply alter the way we look at others. It changes how we understand ourselves and the world. As Stephen said, if you erased the forty-five years that have passed since his mother handed him his first Cowboys lunch box, if you erased his fandom: "I would be something less than I am now. I would be a different person." Fandom changes who we are.

Fig. 6.2

What is the effect of such change, at scale? By adding complexity to our social identities, fandom has the effect of reducing bias toward out-groups, promoting complex thought processes, increasing trust, and shifting fans' social attitudes, regardless of their political ideologies. To gauge the magnitude of fandom's "depolarizing" effect, we put it to the test: We asked Democrats and Republicans how they felt about each other, using an adaptation of the feeling thermometer — the same one Lillianna Mason used. As expected, Democrats have "cooler" feelings toward Republicans, and vice versa. But look at the trend along the Value scale. Once again: the bigger the fan, the "warmer" the feelings toward their "opposition."

Democrats' Feeling Towards Republicans
(n = 6,300)

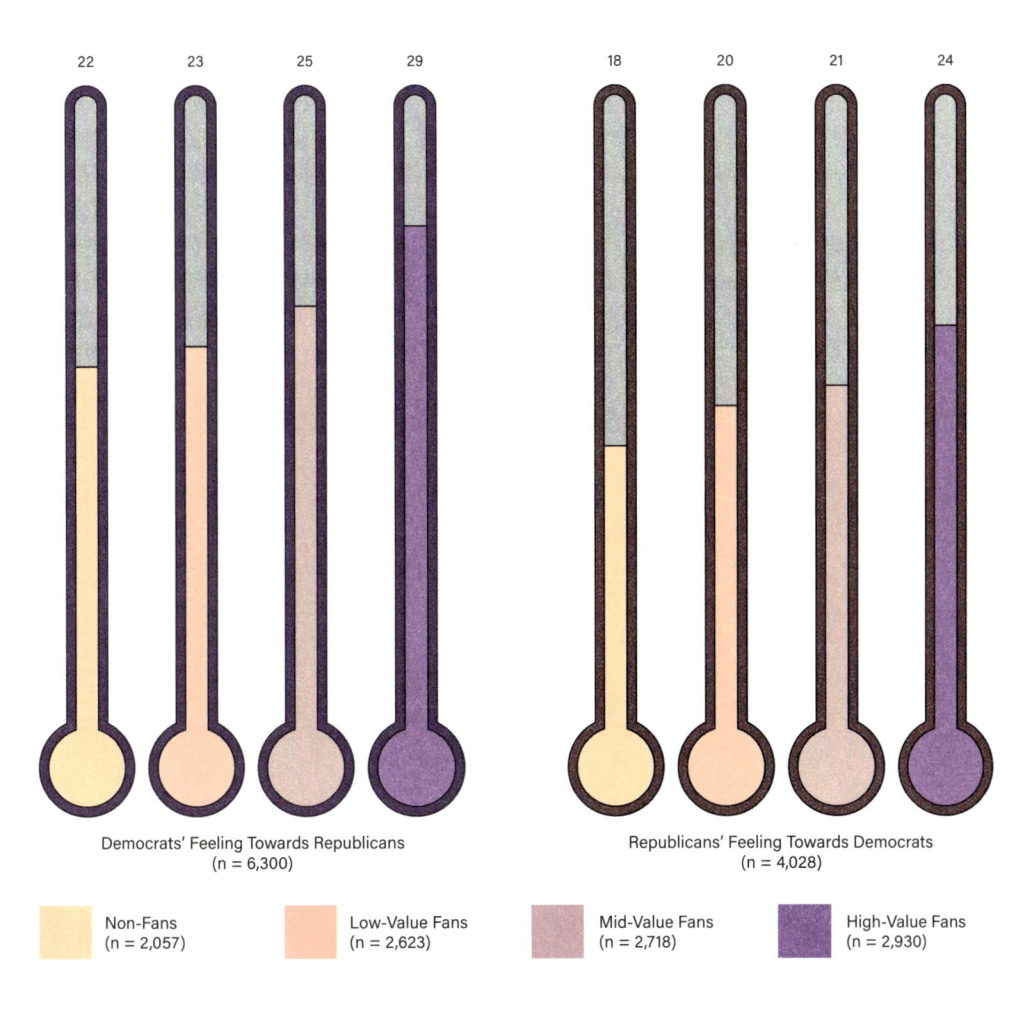

- Non-Fans: 22
- Low-Value Fans: 23
- Mid-Value Fans: 25
- High-Value Fans: 29

Republicans' Feeling Towards Democrats
(n = 4,028)

- Non-Fans: 18
- Low-Value Fans: 20
- Mid-Value Fans: 21
- High-Value Fans: 24

Non-Fans (n = 2,057)
Low-Value Fans (n = 2,623)
Mid-Value Fans (n = 2,718)
High-Value Fans (n = 2,930)

6.2 **Feeling Thermometer rating for opposing party.** N = 10,328.
Q: How would you rank these identities? Please rank from most important "1" to least important "8".

So, even when it comes to these most polarized of identity categories, possessing a cross-cutting fan identity can have a measurable impact on our attitudes toward one another. We wholeheartedly believe that the healing our country needs will not come from the top down. It will happen at the grassroots level, one by one, among individuals willing to see, hear, understand, and validate each other; individuals capable of navigating ambiguities and contradictions; individuals open to seeing the world not through their own myopic lenses but through a more colorful prism. And because of the power of fandom to soften the otherwise hard edges of our current climate, we also believe that fans can lead the way.

07 Embrace Your Fandom

When we first set out to understand the fan experience, we certainly didn't expect to become advocates for fandom's ability to address widespread social problems like loneliness and polarization. More than anything, we were dissatisfied with the prevailing discourse around fandom. It felt incomplete. We knew — based on our own experience — that fandom offered us something more profound than conventional thinking prescribed, but we could not articulate exactly what that was. So, we started pulling at threads, revealing insights that would help us piece together a truer picture of how fandom operates.

So, how does fandom operate? By this point, it should be clear that the driving force motivating all fan engagement is social connection. Once we tuned in to this insight, we could not unsee it. The social benefits of fandom sprang up everywhere. We saw our phones light up more often in the fall, with fantasy football trade offers and "Did you see that?" group texts. We realized that our New York friend networks really do get activated when the Yankees make the post-season. We saw how our "most frequently called friends" list shifts slightly as the sports calendar clicks over from football to basketball season. We saw all the fan activity for what it was: a seasonal cycle of social engagement. We saw the fandom flywheel in motion.

We also started to use sports proactively, for specifically social ends. We were inspired to always send that text about that game. We went out of our way to acknowledge the stranger on the street sporting our favorite team's gear. We started taking our kids to more games. We accepted every invite to every pick-'em pool — because we were aware that this sort of activity results in meaningful social interactions that make us happier, more satisfied, more optimistic, and more engaged with the people around us.

Our journey — over many years — has been something akin to a religious conversion. Today, we're not just converts but evangelists, spreading the good news about fandom. Although the positive case for fandom is rarely made, our research has shown clearly and consistently that fandom has a net positive effect on individuals and communities. And we therefore argue that increasing the number of sports fans and deepening their engagement will have a positive impact on society at large. This is a big idea that imbues our work with a true sense of purpose. So, while we didn't set out to become advocates, that's the position we find ourselves in today.

If you peel back the layers, what we're ultimately advocating for is more belonging. That's the end; sports are simply the means. We are social creatures by nature, and social connection is a critical component of a happy, fulfilled life. In aggregate, happier, more fulfilled people make for a happier, more fulfilled society. That inherent potential is why we are asking you, dear reader, to embrace your fandom.

A SOCIAL SUPERCONDUCTER

Sports fandom operates as a social superconductor because of its scale. Simply put, we believe that sports are the greatest galvanizing force for social connection in human history. That might sound grandiose. But if you think about it, what else could make the list? Religion? Maybe. But the fact that we could even make the comparison between sports and religion is telling in and of itself. That's the scale we're talking about, and that's what makes this story so important. If sports fandom can meaningfully improve the day-to-day quality of peoples' lives, and a critical mass of people already engage in fandom, then we're looking at a force that can move the wellness needle at a population level. Pause for a moment to let that sink in. When we think about solutions to pervasive problems like loneliness and polarization, this sort of reach matters.

It's important to note that people can cultivate a sense of belonging through a variety of means. There are many ways to meet people, myriad commonalities to bond over. School, work, and parenting all function as galvanizing agents. So can a shared interest in wine or sneakers or Tarantino movies or reality TV or yoga or CrossFit. But none of them operate at the scale of sports. If we dropped you into a bar anywhere in the country, your chances of bumping into an NFL fan far exceed your chances of meeting, say, a *Game of Thrones* fan. That's admittedly an unfair comparison, and that's the point: nothing compares to the reach of sports. This notion extends beyond borders, too. It's safe to say that you could have meaningful-if-fleeting interactions with taxi drivers in St. Louis, Stockholm, Shanghai, and Sao Paulo by mentioning Lionel Messi. The same is simply not true of Luke Skywalker or Taylor Swift or the Buddha himself.

Why do sports enjoy such scale? First, they're approachable. You don't have to be an expert to talk sports, just like you don't have to be a meteorologist to talk about the weather. Sports offer an easy on-ramp, so even a novice fan can bring up last night's game around the water cooler and spark a conversation that creates connection. They're also versatile: they can facilitate a five-second "fast friend" interaction with a stranger on the street and at the same time they can serve as the foundation of your relationship with your father.

Second, more so than other interests, sports fandom is easy to signal, which creates entry points for conversation anywhere you go. That's just not true of muscle cars or baking or woodworking or any other shared interest that can foster a relationship. It's culturally acceptable — even fashionable — to wear your favorite player's jersey. But if you go to the grocery store dressed like Iron Man, you're bound to get some looks. Wear a Cubs hat while hiking in

Phoenix, though, and you're likely to be acknowledged by a stranger with a high-five or a "Go Cubs!"

Additionally, sports are as close to a neutral ground as we have in our culture today. Sports are non-ideological in nature. Fandom welcomes all, regardless of race, creed, religion, gender, or socioeconomic status. There are no minimum requirements to be a fan: just come as you are. In our polarized world, the fact that sports offer one of the few "safe" spaces for connection and conversation dramatically extends their reach (and usage rate).

The sports world also operates on a reliable, recurring rhythm. Just think about baseball. Major League teams play 162 games every season, each one offering an opportunity to get together, make a call, or just send a text. And there's always another season on the horizon. This cadence means that fandom is continually renewed. Sports are steadfast, the gift that keeps on giving, continually providing fodder for frequent and consistent social interactions that are good for you, good for others, and good for society.

Consider a sports fan's annual calendar: the year begins with college bowl games and the College Football Playoff, quickly followed by the NFL Playoffs, culminating in what is essentially a national holiday, the Super Bowl. Next up, March Madness captivates the nation for a few weeks, transitioning right into MLB's opening day. While you're riding the early waves of baseball season, the NHL and NBA Playoffs rise and crescendo, carrying you through May and June. And then, come August, you're preparing for your fantasy football draft. October keeps you busy, tracking the MLB Playoffs, keeping stride with the NFL and college football seasons, and hailing the arrival of the NHL and NBA seasons. That's your cycle, every year, with soccer, NASCAR, tennis, golf, and MMA events peppered in between. In short: there's no break from sports. You're never more than a few weeks away from some major event and the social interaction associated with it. Sports fans tap into a constant flow, all year long.

What's more, the sports-based interactions embedded in that reliable calendar encompass the entire range of human emotion. Fans are not simply trading stats and trivial hot takes; they're riding emotional waves together. The hope, the expectation, the elation, the disappointment, the frustrations, the trade rumors, the Cinderella stories, the injury updates, the thrill of victory, and the agony of defeat: all are shared emotional experiences that strengthen bonds, forge deep connections over time, and elevate our emotional intelligence. Win or lose, sports ultimately offer fans an opportunity to connect. It doesn't matter whether we're celebrating or commiserating: we reap the benefits of fandom just the same.

Amidst these multitudes of emotions lies a paradox: sports matter so much to so many, and also not at all. They offer us an experience of competition, with stakes that are simultaneously meaningful and inconsequential. Those tears shed in the stands by a pack of dejected 12-year-olds after their team suffers a shock defeat are as real as the sun that will greet them the very next morning. This inherent contradiction cultivates a playfulness — you can freely trash talk a friend who supports a rival team, all while recognizing that the on-the-field rivalry only serves to deepen your off-the-field friendship.

MODEL BEHAVIOR

Jamie Wedel knows well the social power of sports. Growing up in small-town-Michigan in the 1970s and 80s, Jamie played baseball, football, and hockey. "I wasn't super stellar at any of them," he told us, but at his high school, where kids gravitated into seemingly impenetrable cliques, athletics enabled him to move between them, befriending people from all groups.

After graduation, Jamie attended the University of Michigan, earning a degree in computer science and deepening his lifelong, generations-deep connection to the Wolverines. Put it this way: thirty years after his college graduation, Jamie's Zoom handle is "Wolverine." His stage name when he plays guitar: also Wolverine. We first met Jamie in the fall of 2018 during a college football focus group. He stood out to us not only because of his obvious enthusiasm for college football, but because he was clearly a social connector: he kept everyone included in the conversation, and by the end of the session, he had invited the whole group to join his family's college football pool.

In a follow-up interview after the focus group, we asked Jamie if we could spend a college football Saturday with him, to witness his fandom in action. That adventure began at his home, in the suburbs of Atlanta, Georgia. There he greeted us at the door, accompanied by a dog wearing a Michigan jersey, whom Jamie had trained to bark whenever anyone yells, "Go Blue!" As we entered his home, ESPN's College GameDay was already blaring on his enormous TV. But that was only one of many screens in the room: also in play were one other TV, a computer monitor, an iPad, and an iPhone. Somehow, Jamie managed to keep his eye on the Michigan game while simultaneously following several other games, and — most importantly — remaining thoroughly engaged with friends and family members across the country. It quickly became clear to us that Jamie was watching multiple games, gathering snippets of each, so he could use them to connect with his family and friends. The games appeared to be fodder for conversation. When we ran that theory by him, he confirmed it: "Bingo."

In fact, connection was the impetus behind Jamie's college football pool. Somewhere around 2015, with his family spread out around the country and his parents aging, Jamie decided he wanted to do more to keep in touch with them. He started with his father, Jerry: "My dad is a man of few words, but sports has been his language. So, it started as a generational thing, just the three of us: my dad, my son, and me. We would make some picks on three or four games. Then my daughter made some picks. Then my mom, Marilyn, she's always been a sports fan, so she's like, 'I want to play.' Mom doesn't know as much about football, so it made sense to implement the spread. So, we put together this little worksheet, and we decided, 'Let's play five or ten games,' and it just kind of grew from there."

He goes on: "My wife won one year, my mom won one year, my sister won one year, my daughter won one year. I've never won a full season, but that's not my goal. My goal is bringing people together, enjoying the experience together."

There's no money involved in the pool, but competition runs high. What are the stakes? Bragging rights amongst the participants by way of a little crown icon next to your name. "We've had discussions about money," Jamie told us. "But my nephew plays and some kids play, and I don't want that to be the lesson that they learn, that the only reason you do things is for money. You do it for the camaraderie."

The real reward comes in strengthening the bonds between family members. "That's our base platform that we communicate on, that we all come together on, that we see eye to eye on." This is a theme that runs through fandom: even in families with complicated dynamics, sports are the holding ground for uncomplicated conversations, shared emotions, and playful competition. As Jamie said, "It's hard to get it wrong. We're all on the same wavelength."

For Jamie's social network, the college football pool is the anchor for interactions, but the text thread is the ship. That's where all the action happens. Being in the pool gets you in on the text thread, where the dozens of fans Jamie has brought together share articles, photos, personal stories, and the friendly banter you would hear if they were gathered in Jamie's house, watching a game. Unlike the pool, the text thread is not limited to college football. It lights up whenever something notable takes place in the wide world of sports. In other words, it lights up a lot.

RECOGNIZE THE POWER

Fans like Jamie may recognize fandom as a positive social force, but they don't always understand the nuances of its power. Neither did we, until we thought more critically about it. Today, we understand that fandom facilitates personal relationships, increases social interactions, expands social networks, fosters a sense of belonging, helps people connect with something larger than themselves, and creates heightened levels of openness and trust. Fandom offers a balm for the all-too-familiar pain of loneliness and polarization. While some people are aware of fandom as a social superconductor — and leverage it as such — many more engage in fandom without fully understanding the motivations behind their choices or the cascade of benefits they receive. As a result, when they try to articulate their passion for sports to others, the conversation falls flat. Here's a typical scenario:

Non-Fan: "Do you have to spend every Sunday watching football?"

Fan: "Yeah. It's what we do in our house."

Non-Fan: "It's just football. Why does it matter?"

Fan: "We're Raiders fans. We've gotta root for the team."

Non-Fan: "Can't you miss this one Sunday? I mean, it's just one game.

Fan: "We bleed silver and black. We gotta support the team."

Non-Fan: [Insert eyeroll] "It's just a silly game!"

In a conversation between fans and non-fans,

that line — "It's just a silly game!" — signals an impasse. Instinctively, a fan knows it's more than "just a game." But how can he or she articulate the "more than" to a non-fan? Before we began our inquiry into fandom, we'd shrug and agree to disagree. But now we see it differently. Today's conversation might look more like this:

Non-Fan: "Do you have to spend every Sunday watching football?"

Fan: "Yeah. It's the one time every week that we drop everything else and make time for each other. Things haven't always been great for my family, but football is something we have always agreed upon. Everybody is there, everybody is engaged: Dad wears his lucky jersey, Mom makes the seven-layer dip, Uncle Matt and Aunt Jeanine always show up, the neighbors usually drop by. Football is the glue that holds us all together, no matter what."

Rather than reaching an impasse, conversations that lay bare the inner workings of fandom can invite non-fans into the world that fans know and love. We hope that understanding the power of fandom will inspire you to use this tool for all its worth, just as Jamie does with his family. In his words, "It's a bonding experience. It's a medium to communicate and connect. It's something we can all watch, something we can all relate to. There's a vibrational energy that's shared that you all tap into. It's extraordinary." Even when they're apart, his family feels like they're together.

LEVERAGE THE POWER

Once you recognize the power of fandom, we hope you will leverage it in your own life. The flywheel of fandom often spins without our awareness. But when we become conscious of it and intentionally lean into it, the power of fandom — and its benefits — increases exponentially. Need an injection of social activity in your life? Invite a couple friends over to watch a game. Feeling disconnected from your peers at work? Start a fantasy league. Need to break the ice with a new client? Ask her about the Roll Tide sticker on her laptop. Want more time with your kids? Take them to a game. Missing your family? Start a group text about your hometown team. Want to break out of your social bubble? Talk to the people sitting near you at the ballpark. Got a friend you've lost touch with? Text her and ask if she watched last night's game.

Fandom offers a spectrum of behaviors — from low-effort to high-, from nodding at strangers who signal their fandom, to accepting an invitation to a pick-'em pool, to organizing a tailgate party, to becoming the commissioner for your fantasy league. Wherever your fandom expresses itself, lean into it, and see where it takes you. You may be surprised.

For Jamie, the football pool has grown far beyond his original intent. No longer simply a meeting place for family, it's become a community of sports fans from all walks of life. Why? Because Jamie invited them in. "As you add people into the group," he said, "they become part of the family." He has invited his primary care physician, an extra he met on a movie set, a guy who uses a Purdue logo as his avatar on a music trivia game he sometimes plays. When someone shows an interest in college football, Jamie opens the door: "Hey, we run this pool ..." That sets off a chain reaction. New members bring in their friends, and each addition brings more opportunities for social interactions. Says Jamie, "We realized it had legs when everybody seemed to get more engaged, saying, 'I'm watching games that I never did before' or 'I'm more into college football than I ever was before.'"

The experience has impacted Jamie's fandom as well. "I can't imagine going back to watching college sports without my friends, without my family, without you [yes, of course we joined] in the pool, without the other members. If you don't have anybody to share it with …" His voice trailed off, as if that wasn't a sentence worth finishing.

SHARE THE POWER

"Sports give you an easy in to make friends," Jamie told us, and fandom builds "a bridge to help people." During the early-days of the COVID-19 pandemic, Jamie used that bridge to form an abiding friendship with his neighbor, Paula.

In the spring of 2020, while much of the country was under "shelter in place" orders, Jamie noticed Paula's husband walking out to their mailbox. They waved to each other, but didn't cross the street, due to social-distancing protocols. A couple days later, Jamie noticed an ambulance at Paula's house. When he checked in to see if the couple needed anything, he learned that Paula had lost her husband to COVID-19.

"She's a friendly person that I could tell was lonely, and my wife really likes her, so it was easy to take over some food." When protocols allowed, the neighbors set up a card table outside their homes to play a round of Rummikub, with an Atlanta Braves game playing in the background. That's when they discovered they had more than proximity in common: they were all baseball fans. From then on, they synched their card-playing with Braves broadcasts, and they added another fan into the mix: Paula's sister, Pam, a retired nurse who had lost her husband three years earlier. Now it's a regular event: "We go over for game night, we put sports on the TV. Now we're texting each other when something happens, like 'Oh my god, did you see Acuña got hurt?'"

As friendship and fandom deepened, propelling each other forward, Jamie reflected on their impact: "I think sports help people through suffering. Sometimes life can be lonely, but if you know the Braves are coming on at 7:05, it's not hard to look forward to it, to give yourself a reason to get excited." It's not the game itself Jamie's looking forward to: it's the social interactions associated with the game.

Plain and simple: if fandom creates a sense of belonging that reverberates through society, then we need to generate more fandom. As fans, we are frontline actors in that mission. The more confident we are in our fandom, the more conscious we are of fandom's power, the more prepared we are to serve as ambassadors, inviting people into our sports families, using fandom to build bridges across social divisions, and activating it to benefit our communities. Think of sports as a tool you can use, and then ask yourself, "Where do I want to deploy this tool?"

At the very least, we hope the insights presented in this book will help you reflect on, understand, and articulate the role sports fandom plays in your life. In those moments when someone challenges — or when you question — your choice to invest in season tickets or lay a bet on your team or watch yet another game with your friends, we hope you will remember exactly what you're investing in and what fandom means to you.

Jamie will be the first to tell you that the real payoff happens when you use sports to foster relationships. What started out as a one-off game night with Paula has become a regular Braves watch party, a thriving group chat, shared trips to games, and rich friendships amongst neighbors. Jamie's not done though. He has his eye on another neighbor. "She can be very skittish about meeting new people. I've been trying to get her to come over. I'm just trying to create unity in the neighborhood."

Imagine if everyone did that.

1. Eddie Vedder was interviewed on Chicago sports radio *670 The Score*, July 13, 2019.
2. The team stopped using the "Redskins" name in 2020, and officially changed their name to the Commanders in 2022.
3. Scott Boras. "Opinion: We Have to Bring Baseball Back." *New York Times*, May 5, 2020.
4. Aristotle, *Metaphysics*, 350 BCE.
5. One thing to note about quantitative research: "how" you ask the question matters as much "what" you ask. A bad question asked to a large sample doesn't make the data reliable. We built our survey with three philosophical principles in mind. First, we created a mix of question types (bi-polar, rating scales, multi-select options, and open-ended) and topics (attitudes and behaviors). Second, following the principle that simplicity leads to accuracy, we asked binary questions whenever possible. Third, we kept in mind that respondents are human — they get tired, they get distracted, they misremember — so we attempted to not cross the fine line between detailed questioning and respondent fatigue.
6. While most sports betting does not resemble the media stereotype, we cannot ignore the risk of problem gambling. For a minority of bettors, compulsive gambling is a substantial issue. As with any potentially destructive behavior, proponents and providers of legalized sports betting must acknowledge problem gambling and embed appropriate safeguards. We hope that betting organizations will refrain from exploiting fans who exhibit addictive behavior patterns and that anyone struggling with problem gambling will seek — and be able to access — help.
7. Jim Collins. *Good to Great*. London, England: Random House Business Books, 2001.
8. Brad Stone. *The Everything Store: Jeff Bezos and the Age of Amazon*. New York: Little, Brown and Company, 2013.
9. When Collins wrote *Good to Great* in 2001, he probably didn't envision a future where DoorDash would reference their operational flywheel as part of their 2020 S-1 filing with the United States Securities and Exchange Commission. The flywheel is now a commonly cited strategic framework leveraged across industries.
10. George Vaillant, Charles C. McArthur, Arlie Bock. "Grant Study of Adult Development, 1938–2000," https://doi.org/10.7910/DVN/48WRX9, Harvard Dataverse, V4, UNF:6:FfCNPD1m9jk950Aomsriyg== [fileUNF]. 2022.
11. Joshua Wolf Shenk. "What Makes Us Happy?" *The Atlantic*, June 2009.
12. Michael E. McCullough, Robert A. Emmons, and Jo-Ann Tsang. "The Grateful Disposition: A Conceptual and Empirical Topography," *Journal of Personality and Social Psychology* 82(1) 2002: 112–127.
13. Morris Rosenberg. *Society and the Adolescent Self-Image*. Princeton, NJ: Princeton University Press, 1965.
14. Vivek Murthy. *Together: The Healing Power of Human Connection in a Sometimes Lonely World*. New York: Harper Wave, 2020.
15. Noreena Hertz. *The Lonely Century: How to Restore Human Connection in a World That's Pulling Apart*. New York: Penguin Random House, 2021.
16. Dan Buettner. *The Blue Zones: Lessons for Living Longer from the People Who've Lived the Longest*. Washington, DC: National Geographic, 2012.

17. Daniel W. Russell. "UCLA Loneliness Scale (Version 3): Reliability, Validity, and Factor Structure." *Journal of Personality Assessment* 66(1) 1996: 20–40.
18. Cigna. *Loneliness and the Workplace: 2020 US Report.* Bloomfield, CT: 2020.
19. Joe Keohane. *The Power of Strangers: The Benefits of Connecting in a Suspicious World.* New York: Random House, 2021.
20. Gillian M. Sandstrom and Elizabeth W. Dunn. "Is Efficiency Overrated?: Minimal Social Interactions Lead to Belonging and Positive Affect," *Social Psychological and Personality Science* 5(4) 2014: 437–442.
21. Gillian M. Sandstrom and Elizabeth W. Dunn. "Social Interactions and Well-Being: The Surprising Power of Weak Ties," *Personality and Social Psychology Bulletin* 40(7) 2014: 910–922.
22. Bill Bishop. *The Big Sort: Why the Clustering of Like-Minded America is Tearing Us Apart.* Boston: Houghton Mifflin Harcourt, 2008.
23. Ezra Klein. *Why We're Polarized.* New York: Avid Reader, 2020.
24. Lilliana Mason. *Uncivil Agreement: How Politics Became Our Identity.* Chicago: University of Chicago Press, 2018.
25. Pew Research Center. *Trust and Distrust in America*, July 2019.
26. Gordon H. Allport. *The Nature of Prejudice.* New York: Basic Books, 1979.
27. Thomas Pettigrew and Linda Tropp. "A Meta-Analytic Test of Intergroup Contact Theory," *Journal of Personality and Social Psychology* 90(5) 2006: 751–783.
28. John F. Dovidio, Tamar Saguy, Elze Ufkes, Daan Scheepers and Samuel Gaertner. "Inclusive Identity and the Psychology of Political Change," in *Social Psychology and Politics*, Ed. Joseph P. Forgas, Klaus Fiedler, William D. Crano. New Jersey: Rutgers, 2015. 289–306.
29. Brené Brown. *Braving the Wilderness: The Quest for True Belonging and the Courage to Stand Alone.* New York: Random House, 2017.
30. Marilyn Brewer and Sonia Roccas. "Social Identity Complexity," *Personality and Social Psychology Review* 6(2) 2002: 88–106.

This is a book about community, so it is a great pleasure for us to acknowledge the contributions of many people to this effort. First and foremost, our wives—Tammy Sikorjak and Ghislaine Valenta—who have been loving, patient, and supportive partners. And to our kids—Julian and Alex Sikorjak and Sonny, Moe, and Betty Valenta—who grounded us and provided the motivation to follow through.

To the fans who shared their stories with us: Greg Armstrong, Lindsay Camfield, Nick Camfield, Stephen Chukumba, Garry Dervishian, Chris Falwell, Meghan Hartnett, Britanni Johnson, Jennifer Klovee-Smith, Kyle Miles, Marco Moretti, Sean Oliver, Jennifer Pratt, Brandy Thigpen, and Jamie Wedel. You are the book. Your enthusiasm and generosity made this possible. And to Teddy Liouliakis from Open House Lofts, who connected us with many of these fans, and has been a constant source of entertainment.

We owe a debt of gratitude to our colleagues at FOX Sports who have supported this project: Charlie Dixon, Michael Mulvihill, Mark Silverman, and Eric Shanks. In particular, Michael Mulvihill, who has approached every conversation on the topic with curiosity, pushed our thinking every step of the way, and graciously offered his eloquence to the opening pages.

We owe an equally great debt to Austin McGhie and Sharon Otterman, who recognized our abilities before we did, and whose belief in us early in our careers has propelled us forward.

To our partners at Silicon Valley Press: Vanessa Campos, Joe DiNucci, Cheryl Dumesil, Atiya Dwyer, and Susan Goldberg. Thank you all for your partnership. In particular, Cheryl Dumesil, whose energy, creativity, and artful command of language brought the necessary clarity to our ideas.

To our partners at Doubleday and Cartwright: Aaron Amaro, Maria Chimishkyan, Marcial Cordova-Sanchez, Christopher Isenberg, Marjeta Morinc, and

Jordi Ng. Thank you for pushing us in the right design direction and lending your sensibility to our work. In particular, Jordi Ng, whose aesthetic brought our thinking to life in inspiring ways.

To the many people along the way who have elevated our thinking. Charlotte Vansgaard, who helped us initially craft the idea "to be a fan is to be a part of a community" and then nudged us gently in the direction of belonging. Rick Fernandez, who took the time to read several drafts and acted as a valuable sounding board and constant source of encouragement. Bob Keyser, whose early, off-the-cuff suggestion to include more fan stories proved prescient. Damion Thomas, who provided useful guardrails for navigating issues of race. Richard Wolffe, whose book-writing wisdom was the inspiration that got us started and whose thoughtful critiques made our work better. Rodney Withers, who has been a trusted confidant and an ongoing source of insight throughout the many book-writing stages. Kesu James, who enthusiastically engaged with our ideas and helped us work through potential book titles. Arthur Brooks, Reece Brown, and Candice Gayle, who were the first people outside our inner circle to engage with these ideas, and whose embrace helped us realize that our thinking could break through. Dan Buettner, who lent his credibility and expertise, and always pushed us to put theory into practice. David Holander, who has generously offered his good humor and insight to this project. Ben Shields, who inspired us to start thinking big. And finally, to Graham Valenta, who has been our consigliere throughout the journey.

Ben Valenta is the SVP of Strategy & Analytics for FOX Sports. In his previous life as a consultant, he advised an incredible array of clients, including: Nike, the NFL, Anheuser-Busch InBev, YouTube, ESPN, National Geographic, MSNBC, NBC News, Livestrong, the New York Knicks, and the New York Rangers.

David Sikorjak is the founder of Dexterity Consulting, a strategy and analytics consultancy that artfully blends research, analysis, and empathy to transform how brands think. Prior to that, he was an executive at Publicis, NBC, and Madison Square Garden.

Fans Have More Friends

Copyright © 2022 Ben Valenta and David Sikorjak

No part of this book may be reproduced, or stored on a retrieval system, or transmitted in any form or by any means, electronic, mechanical, photocopying, recording, or otherwise, without express written permission of the publisher.

Published by Silicon Valley Press, Carmel, CA
siliconvalleypress.net

ISBN 9798985842814 (pbk)
ISBN 9798985842821 (ebook)
Library of Congress Number: 2022906657

Printed in Italy

EDITOR
Cheryl Dumesnil

COPYEDITOR
Susan Goldberg

ART DIRECTION & DESIGN
Doubleday and Cartwright
Jordi Ng

LITHOGRAPHY
Marjeta Morinc

COLOR PROFILE
Pantone Violet 0631, Pantone 811,
Pantone Yellow 0131, Black

PRINTER
Musumeci, Italy

PAPER
Ispira Grigio Londra
Munken Print Cream